THE WAY IT WAS

THE WAY IT WAS

Tales from a Policeman's Notebook

by

RAY GIBBON

with sketches by
Michael Gent

The Memoir Club

© Ray Gibbon 2010

First published in 2010 by
The Memoir Club
Arya House
Langley Park
Durham
DH7 9XE
Tel: 0191 373 5660
Email: memoirclub@msn.com

British Library Cataloguing in
Publication Data.
A catalogue record for this book
is available from the
British Library

ISBN: 978-1-84104-217-6

Typeset by TW Typesetting, Plymouth, Devon
Printed by J F Print, Sparkford, Somerset

Dedication

To my four grandchildren:
Richard, Eleanor, Matthew and William

To colleagues past and present

Contents

List of Illustrations

Foreword

I have been privileged to know Ray Gibbon for many years. He was a fine policeman and a superb dog handler. Together with his faithful partner Rebel he provided a reassuring presence on the streets of County Durham. Rebel was an excellent police dog who was awarded a prize for the best operational police work in the county, a tribute to both Rebel and Ray. They were a wonderful team and continued to enjoy many happy years both at work and home.

This thoroughly enjoyable memoir is a warm-hearted and nostalgic collection of tales from the past. It tells of a time when a community policeman was exactly that, a valued and well-respected member of the local community. Ray is a great story-teller and his anecdotes are always highly amusing, even when they are at his own expense, such as the two times in a row he found himself breaking in to a house to try and resuscitate the lady inside only to find she was merely sleeping with her hearing aid turned off. The many colourful characters that Ray comes across all benefit from his patience, wisdom and good-sense. They also all went into his notebooks and are remembered fondly in most cases. As Ray said when questioned about how many arrests he and Rebel made: 'It is sometimes an admission of failure to have to make an arrest.' Advice that younger generations of police officers would do well to listen to. Ray's memories are a good-humoured and clear-eyed glimpse of the past but they contain lessons for the present and the future about the importance of community and the role of the policeman within it.

A long and distinguished policing career was followed by Ray continuing to do his best to help those less fortunate than him; he helped the Samaritans and was a member of the Citizens Advice Bureau for twenty years. He became a Durham City Councillor, representing Witton Gilbert for 16 years. Ray had the honour of serving as Mayor of Durham in 2003/2004 and continued to demonstrate his compassion and good judgement in that role. In 2008 he was awarded the highest honour that Durham City Council can bestow and made an Alderman of the City. A fitting tribute to his years of selfless service on the behalf of the people of County Durham.

Jon Stoddart QPM BA(Hons),
Chief Constable of Durham Constabulary

Preface

I was born on 24 September 1929 in the village of Witton Park in the south of County Durham. It had come to life as a boom town in the early 1800s when it was reputed to have one of the largest steel works in Europe. Workers moved there from all over the United Kingdom. Unfortunately by the early 1900s it had all collapsed and the village entered into decades of deprivation and hardship. Despite this the village retained its sense of community and those who were born and brought up there maintained a fierce sense of pride in the village and loyalty to it. No matter how far they moved away they always referred to it as home. A few loyal and hardy souls refused to let it die and today it is in a sense being reborn. However that is another story told elsewhere.

I was one of three boys, my elder brother Dennis preceding me by nine years, my younger brother, Joe, coming three years after me. Our father was a miner working in the local drift mines. He had two ambitions: the first one was to ensure that his sons did not follow him down the mine; the second to have his own farm. He succeeded in both; Dennis joined the RAF as a boy entry, became a flight engineer with Bomber Command and spent three years as a prisoner of war. Joe became a Methodist minister. Dad eventually worked his way out of the pits and rented a forty-acre farm. However the pit still claimed him, he died at the age of fifty-six, finally losing a hard-fought battle with the coal dust that coated his lungs.

My parents were staunch Methodists and I viewed the congregation of our chapel as an extension of our family. Eventually I became a local preacher and now hold my certificate for forty years' service as a local preacher.

At the age of five I entered the local council school and remained there until I was fourteen. Two weeks after I left school I left home to begin my working life. I went to 'live in' and work on a farm at Wolsingham. The Wearmouth family, a typical hard-working warm-hearted Dales family farmed Ashes Farm. My career in farming peaked when I became a farm manager on a two-hundred acre farm in Worcestershire. I returned home when my father died in 1956. Temporarily unemployed and having no desire to return to farming I spoke to our local policeman (PC Bill Kyle) who had also been a friend of my father. He suggested that I join the police force; I took his advice and have never regretted it. I took another decision in 1956, I married Margaret Allen, another decision I have never regretted.

During my police career I was in three forces. I joined the Durham County Constabulary in 1956. In the 1960s, I am not too sure of dates, the county force was amalgamated with the surrounding borough forces and became the Durham Constabulary. Finally in the 1970s I was stationed at Whickham in Gateshead Division when the new conurbation of Tyne and Wear was born which was policed by the newly formed Northumbria Police Force so I became a Northumbria Policeman.

My police career began at Newby Wiske Police Training School. I was the only member of my syndicate who had never been in the armed services. This swiftly became apparent when we did our first drill period. After about five minutes the Drill Sergeant brought us to a halt and bellowed at the top of his voice, 'O my God I've got a b****y farmer.' To the members of that syndicate I was 'farmer' to the end of my service.

My training being over I was posted to West Hartlepool, a probationer training division noted for its discipline. It was here that I was reported for my first disciplinary offence. I had been detailed to York Road beat and was walking my beat when I saw one of my colleagues, Tom Scales, on the other side of the road and nipped across to have a word with him. Unfortunately as I got to the other side I was spotted by Duty Inspector McCabe. Noted for his strictness, he reported me for deserting my beat. I received a superintendent's caution and was warned re my future conduct. I learnt my lesson and some twenty-two years later, having learned to be more careful and observant received my Long Service and Good Conduct Medals.

After my probation I was sent to a detached beat in the Ferryhill Section of Durham Division. At this time Ferryhill was a thriving mining town, dominated by the two main collieries, Dean and

Chapter, and Mainsforth, which were flanked by several drift mines. I have been reminded of this recently whilst reading accounts of armed robberies and terrorists. One of our duties was to act as escort for the colliery pay wagon. Every Friday morning I or one of my colleagues would meet a colliery wagon, with two miners as escort, outside the bank at 8.0 a.m. Two cash boxes containing the week's pay would be put in the back of the wagon. We would then drive to the colliery office where we would be locked in for the rest of the day whilst the office staff put up then handed the pay packets out through two small windows. The whole procedure was carried out under the watchful eyes of the colliery clerk and under-manager. I do not think that anyone ever gave serious thought to the fact that we could be robbed.

An even more important and dangerous duty was 'guarding the bridges'. The Royal family would often travel from London to Balmoral, always by train, always overnight. Every bridge which the train travelled over or under had to be guarded. The main north/south line passed through our section so we were responsible for several bridges. My bridge was in the middle of farmland about a mile from the road. Only farmers used it to access their land. We were given the time (approximate) that the Royal train would pass through the area. It was a two-mile walk from my home to the bridge. You took up your post armed to the teeth with truncheon, handcuffs and torch until the train thundered past then walked back home, picked up the phone and solemnly informed the town office man that the Royal train had passed safely through. What I would have done had anyone attempted to blow up the bridge I do not know and no one ever told me. Whenever questions were asked about such matters we were told to use our initiative.

The Chief Inspector I/C Dog Section who thought that my experience working with collie dogs on the farm would make me an ideal candidate for an expanding Dog Section approached me. Unless you have worked with dogs you can have no conception of the affection and rapport that can develop between dog and man. It is said that actors should not appear with animals or children, as they are apt to steal the show. Very much the same could be said about policemen and dogs. My colleagues were apt to treat Rebel as the senior partner. When we were called out through the night the town office man would ask me if I would mind giving Rebel a knock then give him a lift to wherever his services were required.

After four years I returned to detached beat duties at Witton Gilbert. The Chief Constable (that wonderful man, Alec Muir) decreed that Rebel should be taken off active service and stay with me. This was one of the happiest times in my service so much so that when Mr Muir decreed that I be made Sergeant and sent to take charge of the Dog Section at Gateshead my family was most unhappy. I promised we would return to the village to live and this we eventually did and I commuted from the village to Whickham where the Dog Section was based.

After three years I asked for a transfer back to beat duties, which was always my first love. I was transferred to Whickham Sub-Division as Shift Sergeant on beat duties. I retired from there in 1984 with twenty-eight and a half years service having reached the age of fifty-five which was the compulsory retiring age for constables and sergeants.

After retiring I spent my time in voluntary work with several organizations, Samaritans, Victim Support, CAB (twenty years). I eventually became a Durham City Councillor and had the honour of being Mayor of the city in the year 2003/2004, and was made an Alderman of the City in 2008.

When I first joined the force it was customary to hand completed pocket books to your sergeant who would check it (no blank spaces or crossings out), sign it then hand it back to you for safe keeping. When you retired you had to hand back in your entire collection of pocket books. I have often seen retired officers placing thirty years of their lives on the office counter and walking away without so much as a backward glance. Sometime in the early seventies someone decided this was not right and that completed books would be handed in and kept in proper safe custody. I am told it has cost many thousands of pounds to store them and employ clerks to file and record them. Such is progress. When I retired no one asked me about pocket books and I never thought about them. Some three years after I retired I tripped over a cardboard box in our attic; the rest, as they say, is history. Many people have said the stories, which have appeared in our village magazine and then *Copper Plate,* the Durham County Police magazine should be published in book form. I am not so sure. However I have finally decided to take the plunge and publish.

I hope the book will bring back memories, and a smile, to my older colleagues, provide a little pleasure to whoever may read it, and perhaps most important, give my younger colleagues a glimpse of other days.

Ray Gibbon
Summer 2009

CHAPTER 1

Mr and Mrs Davies or Two Ordinary People

HE WAS A QUIET RESERVED MAN (but well liked by his neighbours and workmates) about 5 feet 9 inches, thin build and going grey. He liked to go walking in the fields near their home; he had no hobbies. He enjoyed a pint and a game of dominoes at the club but was not what you would call a 'regular'. There was nothing special or noticeable about him, nothing that stood out. She was a little short of her husband's height, slim rather than thin. Always neatly dressed she had a soft voice that had little of the local dialect in it. My mother would have described her as 'lady-like'; she was equally liked and respected by her neighbours. Both in their early sixties they had been married for forty years and had lived in the same upstairs flat for the whole of that time. It was in a street of terrace-type houses near to the banks of the Tyne. There were no children although they had a niece and nephew who they doted on, him especially. She had never worked outside the home; he had worked at Vickers (just across the river) for forty years. They were typical of the type of working-class folk who had helped to make England great. Good manners were essential and proper codes of behaviour.

They went through this life without creating so much as a ripple on its surface. When the ripples came they were not of their making unless you could blame them for growing old. Mr Davies's works manager sent for him. The great day had come: he was due to retire and collect his well-earned pension, have a well-earned rest. Mr Davies was not so sure. For forty years he had led an organised life, most of his thinking had been done for him. Now suddenly he was going to have to organise and fill his days. It was not something he looked forward to. Within a few weeks of retiring the letter came from the council saying they had at last come to the top of the housing list. They had been allocated a council house. It was only about half a mile away in distance but a great leap in their circumstances. Mrs Davies looked forward to it; there was central heating and double-glazing, a modern kitchen. There was also a garden, which would give him something to do. For some reason he never 'took to it'.

At 9 a.m. on a cold winter morning I was thinking of putting the kettle on and opening my sandwiches. Eric appeared in my office door, 'I've got these two elderly women in the office Sarge, one of them wants to report her husband missing. There's no one to deal with them.'

'How long has he been missing?' I asked.

'Since about three yesterday afternoon.' I looked at the sleet and rain running down my office window.

'You had better bring them along Eric.' So began my acquaintance with Mrs and, in a sense, Mr Davies. I took the usual statement and asked the usual questions, description, clothing, habits. Where did he like to go walking, where did he spend his spare time, what was his mood and so on. I am sure you will have done it. I finally sent them home with the Panda.

I gave my colleague on Dog Section a ring, could he organise his lads. He could and would; once he had despatched them he would send for reinforcements from the adjoining division. Then I had a word with the Chief Inspector. By lunchtime we had eight men plus myself searching the area he used to frequent. I left at 2 p.m. handing over to my relief. At 5 p.m. my phone rang at home, it was the Chief Inspector. 'We have not found him Sarge. I am organising a full search. I want you in at 7 a.m to take charge on the ground.' By 9 a.m. the teams were organised and out searching. The weather was no better, rain and snow showers. Others did door-to-door enquiries, CID visited clubs and pubs. Our colleagues over the river visited his old workplace.

Gradually over the next two days I built up a picture from the information that was fed to me. Mr Davies had become more withdrawn than usual; never one for socialising he had changed from a quiet, somewhat gentle person to being quite morose. One friend tried to get him to go fishing but he simply did not want to know. He had been seen (at different times) standing in his old street looking up at their old flat, and standing on the banks of the Tyne looking across to 'The Works'. After a week the operation was scaled down.

Dog Section went back on their tracks 'just in case'. Panda units checked the allotments once again. Door-to-door enquiries were abandoned. I thought, and still do, that the Tyne had claimed him either by accident or design. I walked along the banks and stood to watch the river, it was in partial flood. It had long ceased to be the leaping, rippling stream from the hills; here it was a swift, brown, sullen flow without so much as a ripple; watching it had a hypnotic effect. The banks were breaking away, the footpath slippy and treacherous under foot. I was glad to get away.

The Chief Inspector asked me to keep an eye on Mrs Davies. I called practically every week. We got to know each other well. She asked about my family, and would tell me about her nieces and nephews. We talked on occasion about Mr Davies, always a quiet man. She said, 'You needed to get to know him, his workmates all liked him.' He was a very caring, thoughtful man and they had always been happy. Very occasionally when I called she would ask, as I went in, 'Is there anything Sergeant?' She knew there was not, it was if she just wanted to be sure. I only once saw tears in her eyes: 'I just wish I knew where he was and he's all right.' I retired a few months later. I called to see her on the odd occasion. Then one day my phone rang it was Mrs Davies's sister. Mrs Davies had died and she thought I would like to know. She gave me the funeral times. The village church was full, an indication of the regard in which they were both held. I did not go to the crematorium or to her sister's home. I thought it best to say my goodbyes at the church. I was happy knowing that now she would not only know where he was but she would be with him again.

CHAPTER 2

The Flood

WHEN THE GOVERNMENT DECIDED to build their new offices on the riverbanks the locals shook their heads and prophesied disaster: that part of the banks, they said, could get seriously wet in winter. The expression 'flood plain' was not then in common usage. The government inspector countered by saying that a great deal of research had been carried out and statistics showed that the possibility of serious flooding was so remote as to be practically non-existent (who was it who said that there were liars, big liars and then there were statisticians?) and certain features had been built into the design to ensure the safety of the building. The foundations had been dug and the brickies were coming up out of the ground when the rains came. It did not rain for forty days and nights but it did rain steadily for several days and nights. The little streams and burns up the dale, filled to overflowing, came burbling and splashing across the moor and down the hills and flung themselves into the river. The river instead of rippling began to roar, it charged down into the city and showing its contempt of governments buried the foundations of the new offices under several feet of water.

Rebel and I were called to the scene about 9 p.m. on Sunday night. We arrived to find a small group gathered around the night watchman's cabin. Fortunately it was situated away from the actual workings and on a slight rise, which kept it above the floodwaters. The group consisted of the night-shift Inspector, Sergeant and Albert (city centre beat man, twenty years' service and a mine of information) and a civilian who was introduced to me as the 'site manager'. The Inspector welcomed me with open arms, as they say, 'Just the lad, Ray,' he said. Then told me the story. The site manager, in view of the worsening weather condition had decided to make a late night visit. He found the door of the site cabin open, the light on but no sign of the night watchman. He had looked at the slippery condition of the ground around the crumbling foundations and had surmised the worst so had informed the police. The Inspector said he

4

had decided to send for me. I was aware of the fact that Rebel and I had something of a reputation for being able to tackle various situations but this I felt was a bit over the top. I spoke in what I hoped was a quiet, controlled manner, 'Inspector, that's a trained dog I have in that van not a porpoise and I will tell you something else, neither of us has webbed feet.' The Inspector said that he fully understood my comments and indeed he would not expect Rebel to work in such adverse conditions. I could have wished that he had the same concern for me. However, did I not have in the van a pair of welly boots and a very powerful hand-held, battery-powered search-light and it was these he would like me to bring into use.

I wandered back to the van reflecting that was probably why he was an inspector whilst Rebel and I remained PCs. I returned to the scene suitably equipped. As I joined them Albert pointed up the road and said, 'He's here, the night watchman, he's here.' We followed his pointing finger to where a tall somewhat portly figure was making his way towards us with the steady studied gait of the inebriated. He stopped in front of our little gathering and addressed the site manager, 'I didn't expect to see you here.' The site manager said, 'That's b****y obvious.' He went on to say that the watchman should consider himself as from that moment to be amongst the ranks of the unemployed and should he care to call at the site in the morning the site manager would personally present him with his cards. The watchman not deigning to reply turned on his heel with drunken dignity and left. We all went our separate ways.

I returned to the scene in the early hours prior to going off duty. I found Albert and the Sergeant in the cabin. Albert had discovered ingredients for making tea (it did not take a lot of doing there was only one cupboard and one small fridge). He was brewing up under the anxious gaze of the Sergeant. I selected a pot from the collection on the bench, God alone knew when they had last had a proper wash. The insides were stained a deep dark brown; however it is a well-known fact that good strong hot tea, like Domestos, kills all known germs. We stood sipping our tea looking out at a brightening sky that showed promise of a better day. The Sergeant took another appreciative sip of his tea and remarked that there was a silver lining to every cloud. The road outside the offices has been flooded, to some extent, on several occasions over the years, so the locals can claim they were right. However, I understand that the water has never entered the building so the government experts can also claim to be right. So that's all right then.

My Dog – Rebel

A regal, sleekly, shining dog
With a wet black nose and pointed ears.
Alert at the slightest sound.
A powerful dog as he walked or ran,
His shoulders and thighs swinging in time with his gait,
Strong muscles rippling through his body
His deep black eyes observe you with a softness never yet achieved by
    humans.
It is a beautiful sight
To see him romping and playing about the countryside.
It is feeding time, and his white teeth flash as he hurriedly devours his
    food.
Teeth that have bitten many a man
He was a police dog.
He slurps his water noisily
As his lolloping tongue flashes
In and out of the water.
Evening comes – he lies quietly head on paws
Looking at the world with soft pleading eyes.

                           (Written by Nigel when 10 years)

CHAPTER 3

The (almost) Midwife

IT WAS A BITTER COLD JANUARY NIGHT, with freezing fog. The town was wrapped in that deep silence that invariably accompanies intense cold in the night hours. Car headlights seemed to swim towards you from a flat, grey sea. Pandas were on stand-by – foot patrol only. It was not, the shift pointed out, fit to turn a dog out. I in turn pointed out to them, gently, that they were not dogs and therefore not entitled to the same privileges, so out you go! At 1 a.m. we were in for early bait (2 a.m. was late bait), huddled around the two-bar electric fire, our little substation boiler was down again. The shift was gathered around a small table, sandwiches in one hand, cards in the other. I puffed my pipe and read the paper – I never was any good at cards. They had offered to teach me but that had happened to me before and I had finished up a poorer but wiser man.

There was a banging at the office door; John leapt up to answer (he was losing) and returned a few minutes later.

'This lad at the door, Sarge, his wife's pregnant.' Bill, the bright spark of the shift, swiftly denied all knowledge. I silenced him. John went on, 'She's expecting a baby.' I shot Bill a glance and he closed his mouth.

'Pregnant women usually are, John.'

'Aye, I know, Sarge but she's expecting it now.' No need to silence Bill – this time a silence had descended, as they say, upon the assembled company.

'He sent for the ambulance about an hour ago; it still hasn't arrived and in this weather . . .' He left the question hanging in the air. A somewhat dishevelled young man appeared in the doorway.

'Could you come now, Sergeant, I have had to leave her on her own, it's just around the corner.' His distress was evident.

'Of course we will, lad.'

I reached for coat and helmet, thinking that with a bit of luck she might have company by the time we got there. I had read of women who had actually delivered their own babies. Anything seemed preferable to having the poor little mite delivered by me and my merry little band. It was then that I realised that my merry little band was fast disappearing; never had I seen them so keen to get back on their beats when it was not fit to turn a dog out. I called for Bill and John to accompany me. We set out, my mind working overtime. I had never been trained in the art of delivering babies – not that that was any excuse, there were so many things I had to do as a policeman that I was never trained to do. I was never trained to type but was supposed to be able to. During my 'office training' (two weeks) the office man had pointed to this machine and said, 'That is a typewriter, son.' He had put a sheet of paper in and told me to type 'the quick brown fox jumped over the lazy dog', or something like that. At the end of the two weeks I was fairly proficient with my two index fingers and the occasional thumb. However, I thought this was going to take a bit more than two index fingers and a thumb, no matter how dexterous. I had, of course, been trained in first-aid but could remember nothing under the heading of 'Babies, Delivering

Of.' Then I remembered the Training Sergeant, after we had passed our exams, telling us that if we ever saw him lying injured, we were to send for an ambulance and not lay so much as a finger on him – not the sort of thing to fill you with confidence.

Not a great deal of demand here for my expertise with the three-cornered bandage, unless it was to keep baby indoors, as it were, until the ambulance arrived. I know I had two children of my own but I had had nothing to do with their coming into this world – in those days expectant fathers were shooed away by maternity nurses, who did not think this was any place for men. I wracked my brain for anything that might be of help. I had seen several films in which the birth of a baby was featured; there was one in particular in which John Wayne featured (if you are too young to remember, maybe you should not be reading this – anyway, ask your Mam or Dad). I remember the doctor being fed copious cups of coffee to get him in a fit state to help but I was stone-cold sober (never more so) so that was a waste of time.

However, there was one thing that was common to all of them – the person in charge was always calling for hot water. It seemed as if gallons disappeared into the room set aside for the event. Just what they did with it, I had not the faintest idea. There did not appear to be much use for it before the event except to wash your hands and half-a-pint would do for that. I did not think that either of the main participants would be thinking of having a bath. Did they, I wondered, dunk baby in it immediately he or she arrived? Did that account for the long wailing baby cry that always emanated from the room to herald the birth? Come to think of it, my own two children were rather red and wrinkled when I first saw them. I even cast my mind back over the Bible story but even there we are simply told that the baby was laid in a manger – just how he got there, or who delivered him, remains shrouded in mystery.

My reverie was interrupted as we arrived at the door. The expectant father ran up the stairs; we heard him telling his wife that he had got the police and that the Sergeant was with them, as if that was an added bonus. Such faith, though touching, was, I felt, badly misplaced.

I went into the bedroom and was greeted with a 'Thank you for coming, Sergeant.' She did not look old enough to be having a baby. I sat down on the side of the bed.

'Is this your first baby?'

'Yes, it is.'

'I have two.' This seemed to exhaust the conversation for a while. 'When did you have the last contraction?' I thought a show of knowledge might help to boost confidence.

'A while before Harry went for you.' I did not like to ask how long a 'while' was.

'I am just going to pop downstairs for a minute but don't worry, we will look after you.' She nodded and smiled. Downstairs, I saw that Bill and John had put the kettle on; I reflected that when men feel helpless in domestic situations that is what they usually seem to do. I went outside where I could not be heard and pressed the wireless button.

'Eric, where is that ambulance?'

'It's on its way, Sarge'

'I know it is, Eric, so is this baby and I would just like to think the ambulance would make it first.'

'Sorry, Sarge, nothing I can do.'

My Inspector (I was later told) was in the office and said she was sure she detected a faint note of rising panic in my voice. I told her (later) that if she could only detect a faint note, she had not been listening very hard.

I went back into the house and started up the stairs.

'Sarge, Sarge' – it was Bill. 'The ambulance is here.' I knew exactly what John Wayne felt like when the cavalry came over the hill. The ambulance men were their usual cheerful, competent selves:

'Come along, love, we will have you there in no time; get your coat on, lad, you will be coming as well.' To us: 'Thanks, lads – be seeing you.'

I left word for the day shift to keep in touch with the hospital. Baby (a healthy boy) finally paraded for duty after lunch. I felt a bit annoyed with him causing his Mam and Dad so much worry, not to mention my blood pressure. I called later that week to remonstrate with him. However, he was asleep and he looked so lovely and peaceful, I had not the heart to wake him up. I popped the traditional piece of silver under his pillow, had a cup of tea with his Mam and departed. I offered up a little silent prayer that I would be the last policeman who worried over what was the best way to get his hands on him.

CHAPTER 4

P.D. Don

WHENEVER WE SPOKE OF HIM phrases such as, 'he does try', 'very willing', 'lovely nature' simply abounded. The trouble was he just could not get anything right. There was the way he moved for a start. Like a typical male teenager lots of movement but no coordination. He walked as if he had rubber joints and his run rapidly deteriorated into an ungainly lollop. His feet (male teenagers again) were an alarming size and totally out of control. His biggest problem was in 'fierce'. He could do 'fierce', he had all the attributes, he was a big lad, the most alarming noises came from his throat (his voice was breaking) and he had all the right facial expressions. The problem was he couldn't be 'fierce', it just was not in his nature. He loved searching, he was good at searching, we just could not get through to him that having found an object he was supposed to stand over it.

He was not supposed to throw it into the air, catch it and chew it. Then there was the trouble over the search for dead bodies. The bodies objected strongly when he stuck his cold nose in their faces and slobbered all over them, he was supposed to stand beside them and shout for assistance. The Chief Inspector I.C. K.9 (think about it) section began to make noises and we began to worry. You see we all liked the lad, you simply could not help it. He was, to put it simply, 'lovable'.

The crunch came the day we sent him yet again into a small wood to find another dead body hoping that this time he would get it right. After a while the body shouted to ask if it was supposed to lie there all day. Where had he gone? We made a swift search and found him socialising with the sheep in an adjoining field. Unfortunately the farmer who was in the next field did not quite see it in that way. The silly man was shouting about worrying, and savaging. In vain did we point out that the lad was simply ambling about amongst the sheep, that he was completely incapable of worrying or savaging anything or anybody. Indeed, we pointed out, the sheep had become far more agitated when he and his dogs had come into the field. All to no avail, we simply could not reason with the man; the Chief Inspector was informed. He was a man of few words. His sole comment was 'He'll have to go.' There was immediate consternation in the ranks, go where, when or more to the point how was he to go? Sensing mutiny the Chief Inspector said we had a week to find, as he put it, a guardian angel who protected sheep socialisers.

It was the following day when the phone rang in the Sergeant's office. It was the Superintendent D Division, a more unlikely angel it would be difficult to imagine, a bit like that one at Gateshead, not a lot of bend in him. The lady, he said, was a close personal friend of his and, he added being a man who liked to get things clear, his wife's. A single retired headmistress who lived in an exclusive bungalow on an exclusive estate (did they I wonder, have exclusive caves?) There had been burglaries in the vicinity and she was a little worried and had decided to have a dog. A friend who had suggested she could have a terrier or a poodle had been swiftly and suitably crushed. The Superintendent's tone, said the Sergeant, seemed to indicate that the lady was expert at swiftly and suitably crushing. What she required was a dog that would not only guard her property but would be a suitable companion when she went rambling. Would he ask the Superintendent if we knew of a suitable applicant for what might be a rather difficult post? The Sergeant, noted for his ability to sell snow to Eskimos and sand to Arabs, said there was just a possibility that we may have such an applicant who was surplus to requirements due to the fact we did not think he was quite up to our very exacting standards.

We visited the lady the following day. We gazed at the large immaculate lawn, at the neat regimented borders and thought of those feet and rubber joints; our hearts sank. The door was answered by a slim lady elegantly clad from hand-tooled leather shoes to beautifully coiffured hair. We introduced ourselves. She flicked her eyes down to our shoes and across to the doormat then with a smile that did not quite reach her eyes invited us in. Two pairs of feet paid an extended visit to the doormat and we entered. It was rather like entering the furniture showroom of a very exclusive shop. The carpet was of the finest Durham could make; in front of the Adam fireplace was an exquisite Chinese rug never meant to be trodden by the feet of ordinary mortals such as ourselves. We looked with feelings akin to horror at two beautifully carved small coffee tables upon each of which stood a very delicate china figurine. We set about a damage limitation exercise. He was, we said, a very large dog. The Superintendent, she countered, had said he was 'obedience trained'. She had no doubt she would quickly learn the necessary skills and commands. We did not doubt it. There was, we said, this little problem of his socialising with sheep when out in the country. She would, she said, see that did not occur. We had no doubts on that either. The Superintendent, her tone indicated that she was accustomed to dealing with those who occupied a higher plain than ours, had indicated that he would come on a week's trial (not the Superintendent). The Sergeant delivered him the next day and spent an hour or so with the lady and her new guard. He had, he said, licked her feet, kissed her hand (not the Sergeant), she had grasped the lead and they had become as one. The Chief Inspector, being of a somewhat suspicious nature, sniffed his breath then offered five to one that she would be on the phone within two days. No one would take him on.

It was five days later when the phone rang, the Superintendent D Division said it was really quite amazing the neighbours could not believe it. He had practically taken over, she referred to him, we winced, as her Donny. We called at the end of the week. The headmistress (single, retired) sat in a chair on the once immaculate lawn. The lad lay at her feet. As we entered the garden he rose, we thought to greet us, but he disappeared behind her chair. She rose, looked fondly down at him, and asked in a gentle tone belied by the look in her eye if our training was very strict. We thought of the hours spent cajoling him and felt betrayed. She walked across the lawn in stocking feet he followed her into the house without so much as a glance at the doormat. We followed, the coffee tables were still there but the figurines had gone, we thought it best not to ask, the Chinese rug had a generous sprinkling of dog hair. We handed over his papers and departed. Neither of them, it was obvious, wanted us to linger.

The good book tells us that God cares for sparrows but take it from me he works miracles with big, clumsy, lovable dogs and single, retired headmistresses.

CHAPTER 5

Little Sam

About 5 feet 5 inches tall and 9 stone, wet through, with a thatch of wavy iron grey hair and a pair of piercing blue eyes that many a budding thespian would have given a year of their life for, of indeterminate age, he spent his days either in his garden or garden shed (of which more later) or walking the village and the surrounding countryside. I never knew him to have a job. The only time he left the village was to go to 'sign on' every Friday. A half-smoked Woodbine was always fixed between the leading fingers of his right hand, I never saw him take a draw at it and am sure that he placed it in an ash tray the last thing at night before he went to bed and replaced it the next morning.

He was both tidy and thrifty, did not like to see things lying about

15

or going to waste. When walking the fields he would carefully remove the odd post or rail that some careless farmer had left whilst fencing. If a turnip was growing across the field path it was carefully tidied away into the little carrier bag that accompanied him on his travels. He would keep a careful eye on any work going on in the village and at the end of the day carefully remove the odd plank of wood, the few tiles or whatever else had been left lying about. It has to be said that toys left out by careless children were always popped back over their parents' garden hedge, although their parents had to be a lot more careful. I did try to get angry with him a couple of times but failed abysmally.

He really came into his own when the new housing estate was being built. Each night and every weekend he conscientiously walked the estate tidying up. Half tins of paint, half bags of cement, half boxes of nails were carefully retrieved, he didn't touch anything that was full that would have been stealing. Half sheets of weyroc, pieces of timber, all found their way into his shed. The shed resembled Dr Who's Tardis. It must have been ten times larger inside than it appeared from the outside judging from what went in and eventually came out. Anyone short of anything to complete a bit of 'do-it-yourself' would make their way to Sam's shed. They were usually quickly 'fixed up', if not with their exact requirement then with something that 'would do'. No money changed hands, Sam would have been offended, but he rarely paid for his beer. There was always a pint over the bar at the club. I did consider having a word with the building site foreman about Sam's tidying up but the day I went to see him he showed me a box of leek plants that that 'canny little feller' had given him. Sam did not grow leeks, no doubt he had done an exchange deal for something he had tidied up from the estate, I thought it kinder to leave things as they were, so said nothing.

I had a spate of break-ins in the village. All bungalows, always at the weekend and obviously the work of juveniles. I was puzzled. There was plenty of mischief amongst the young ones but I was sure no housebreakers. A few enquiries brought up a young man who came from a nearby town to visit his grandparents every weekend. A telephone call to my colleagues left no doubt who my burglar was. He was swiftly brought to book. Unfortunately he had recruited some of my locals to help in his burglaries. I visited their homes recovering items of stolen property. I finished at Sam's to speak to young Sam, a lovely chubby eleven year old. Sam sat in an armchair, Woodbine in position, on one side of the fire, his little dumpy wife on the other side. Young Sam stood in the middle of the fireside rug.

'You got some toys, Sam?'

'Yes.'

'Where are they?'

'In me bedroom.' Sam exploded,

'In thee bedroom! Bye, if I'd known that there would have been bother.' I watched as the Woodbine started towards his mouth hesitated then returned to his side.

'Go and get them, Sam.' There was silence until young Sam returned with a carrier bag, suspiciously like the one his Dad invariably carried. I decided they must have two.

'I understand you got a five pound note, Sam.'

'Yes.'

'Where is it?'

'Me father's got it.' I looked at Sam.

'Is that right, Sam?'

'Aye, well I found him with it. He said he'd found it but Ah didn't believe him so Ah kept it till Ah knew where he'd had it from.' I held my hand out.

'Well now you know, Sam, I'll be having it.' I watched mesmerised as Sam, obviously under great stress, slowly raised the Woodbine to his lips and took a long drag on it (which I swear reduced its size not one whit) and as the smoke trickled out of his nose he gazed at me gently with those blue eyes and said,

'Could tha wait till Friday?' I shouldn't have done but I did. After all, it was Sam.

CHAPTER 6

Little Johnny Thompson

'HAS ANYONE TOLD YOU ABOUT Little Johnny Thompson?'

'No, Coll,' – 'Coll' being PC Colin Robson – twenty-two years' service, broken only by a short interlude when he accompanied General Montgomery from the French beaches to Germany. He had been appointed as my guide and mentor during my first two weeks of service. We were on 9 a.m. to 5 p.m., working the Park Beat in a quiet, respectable area and Coll was taking the opportunity to further my education.

'Don't ever lock him up,' he continued. Now corruption was a word rarely heard in those days, so the thought of anything untoward did not occur.

'He stinks.' Coll was noted for his aversion to wasting breath on words.

18

'When he's drunk, which is every weekend, his language is appalling and if he is in the cells, he shouts and screams all night. The only way you can shut him up is to shoot him and we are not allowed to do that.' Coll's tone of voice indicated that the fact that we were not allowed to shoot Little Johnny was a decision greatly to be deplored.

'Just grab him and take him home – 6 Victoria Street – and throw him in the door – don't go inside.' Coll lapsed into his usual silence.

I met Little Johnny two weeks later, when on night shift on Friday night. I was double with Bill Gray. We were walking down the main street of the bottom end of town. As we approached its junction with Victoria Terrace, Bill pointed to a little figure standing underneath the lamp post on the corner.

'That's Johnny Thompson – he usually stands there when he's had a few; ignore him and with a bit of luck, he'll go home.'

Johnny was about 5 feet 6 inches, and as thin as a lath. He was invariably dressed in a dirty, well-worn donkey jacket which had obviously been made to fit someone about 6 foot tall. The sleeves were rolled back and from underneath peeped two wellie boots. It was rumoured that he had been born with those wellies on and they had simply grown with him – the midwife, it was said, had given him his first and last bath. He was allowed in only one pub, a very rough one down on the sea front. He was allowed to stand in a corner behind the back door, from where he could be served through the bar hatch.

Over the next few months I had two slight brushes with Johnny – on both occasions I had ignored his insults and he eventually went home. The third occasion was not to be so easy. It was 11.30 p.m. on a Saturday night. A mixed group of late-night revellers had had the benefit of a very drunk Johnny's tongue. This time they felt he had gone too far and 'something should be done about him'. I approached Johnny where he stood beneath his lamp post and told him to be quiet and go home. He suggested that I should also go home but not in the words I had used; he went on to give his opinion of me and policemen in general. Enough, I felt, was enough. I moved in on Johnny and reached for the back of his coat collar. Johnny was ahead of me and promptly threw his arms around the lamp post and hugged it to him. It was too late to walk away – a small crowd had gathered to watch the proceedings. They swiftly took sides, some exhorting Johnny to hang on, while others encouraged me to 'get stuck in at him, lad'.

I tugged in vain, first at Johnny's collar, then at his arms. I was beginning to panic slightly when the Divi Car came into view and seeing my predicament, pulled up. Alan, 14 stone of bone and muscle wrapped up in good humour, strolled towards me (he was never one for hurrying).

'Having trouble, Ray? Just a minute.' He gently pushed me to one side and came up behind Johnny and bent over him, his right hand going under Johnny's donkey jacket in the direction of his nether regions. Johnny gave a sudden squeal, let loose the lamp post and fell to the ground. Alan took hold of the back of his jacket and pushed him towards me.

'There you are, Ray – get him home.' I grabbed the back of Johnny's coat collar. Alan disappeared into the car and drove away.

By this time Johnny had regained his feet and breath and began, in a very loud voice, to ask the gathering to witness this act of police brutality. He described in lurid terms what he alleged Alan had done to him. He had, said Johnny, 'crunched a vital part of his anatomy'. I am acutely aware that this could be read by youngsters, so will refrain from going into too much detail. The crowd was coming round to his side – even to the hardened denizens of this part of town, 'crunching' was something that should only be done when *in extremis*, when there was grave danger of losing the battle. It certainly was not on for a 14-stone policemen to do it to the likes of Little Johnny, but they had never had to deal with him.

It was time to go. I pulled at Johnny's coat collar but he dug his heels in while continuing to harangue the crowd. I was saved by a flash of inspiration; throwing caution and all inhibitions to the wind, I reached under the back of that dreadful coat and seized a handful of trouser that I was thankful I could not see and heaved upwards. Johnny was cut off in full flow; a squeaky, gargling sound came out of his throat as he rose up on his toes. Relaxing my grip just enough to allow his feet to come to ground, I began to frog march him down the street. Every time Johnny started to shout, I heaved on his trousers, to be rewarded with the squeaky gargle, followed by blessed silence. We reached number 6, I shoved the door open with my foot (it was never shut – no one was ever likely to go in), gave a final heave to Johnny's trousers and watched as he went down the passage on his toes like an inebriated ballet dancer.

From then on, Johnny and I had an unspoken agreement: if he kept quiet when he saw me approaching, I would keep my hands away from the back of his trousers. It worked very well.

CHAPTER 7

The Whisper

H E'D HAD, SAID THE DI, a 'whisper'. These days, I understand, it is called 'advanced intelligence'. The whisper was that 'the family' were going to break into the pop factory, makers of various soft drinks, in the early hours of Saturday morning, in order to steal the wages deposited in the factory safe. In those far-off days very few people, except those who were in what was known as 'the professional classes' received their wages by cheque. You went to the office on a Friday or Saturday morning, where the wages clerk handed you your earnings in a little brown envelope. You were supposed to take it home to mother or wife, unopened. It was rumoured that there were those who had mastered the art of unsealing the envelope and extracting half-a-crown then re-sealing it. I do not think this is a matter for further discussion – there may be those of a certain age with long memories. The plan, said the DI, was that I and Rebel, accompanied by the local PC, would hide in the factory and pounce on 'the family' when they entered. I gazed at him in consternation. Did not 'the family' have something of a reputation for their expertise in the use of pick-shaft handles and were there not usually four of them?

The DI conceded that this was true but pointed out that one of them remained outside to keep watch, so that left only three and we would have the element of surprise, plus Rebel, who, if it came to battle, was worth at least two men. Not only that, but we would have the wireless on which to summon assistance when we heard them coming, whereupon motor patrols, like John Wayne's cavalry, would gallop to our rescue. The wireless, at that time state of the art, was powered by batteries and housed in a wooden case, the lot weighing about 6 stone. As we were always dropped off away from the premises, that meant it had to be carried for about a quarter of a mile.

Friday night came and we heaved the box across the field behind the factory, letting ourselves in with a key kindly provided by management, who by now were no doubt tucked up in bed. We settled down in the office while Rebel had a stroll around the premises. He returned to stretch himself out at my feet. Bill gazed at him in amazement.

'I thought,' he said, 'he was the watch dog.'

'Don't worry,' I told him, 'he will hear the slightest sound.' Unfortunately Rebel chose this moment to dig himself deeper into the carpet and give a contented snore. Bill was not impressed.

It was 3 a.m. when Rebel, to Bill's amazement, pricked up his ears, stood up and fixed his gaze on the window. I, having greater faith in Rebel than Bill, cautiously lifted a corner of the curtain and peered out. The front gate to the factory, hitherto closed, stood open. Before I had a chance to absorb this, there came the crash of a door being forced open. We rushed to take up our places either side of the door and waited for the footsteps. Bill would then press the wireless switch for reinforcements. They didn't come – instead there was the sound of a wagon engine starting. Bill ran to the window.

'They're taking the wagon.' We galloped down the passage to the front door. It did not occur to us to wonder why anyone would want to take a wagon load of pop. The wagon was going slowly up the ramp towards the gate. I wrenched the passenger door open and leapt in, waving my truncheon and shouting, 'Police!' The driver (he was the only occupant), his hands frozen to the steering wheel, mouth and eyes wide open, was obviously in the process of going into deep shock. The wagon shuddered to a halt and started to roll backwards down the ramp. This put some life back into the driver and he grabbed the hand-brake with his left hand, the rest of his body remaining rigid. Bells started to ring in my head, the horrible realisation beginning to dawn that this had all the appearance of being a monumental mess. I tried to assert some authority – 'if you cannot win it, bluff it', my training sergeant had once said.

'What are you doing with this wagon?' The reply came in steady crescendo.

'What am I doing with it? I am taking it to Carlisle like I do every b★★★★y Saturday.' I suggested that we should go into the office, where we could talk in comfort. Unfortunately, I had forgotten about Rebel. I was reminded of his presence when a howl of agony came from the driver. Rebel, seeing his foot emerge from the wagon door, had promptly clamped his mouth around it and applied pressure as only an Alsatian topping 100 pounds can do. I yelled at Rebel to leave and get down, which, to his credit and disgust, he did. Bill escorted the driver, now reduced to a gibbering wreck, into the office. He said he had not interfered earlier, as he thought Rebel and I had things well in hand. I asked him to cancel motor patrols, which should have arrived by now. He said that would not be necessary, as in all the excitement, he had forgotten to summon them.

That was one of those extremely rare occasions in my life that I was rendered speechless, which was probably just as well. Rebel lay on the concrete looking totally confused and giving me an enquiring look, which was plainly asking why he had been bawled out for doing what he had been specially trained to do. Divisional Office was, reluctantly, informed, the factory manager summoned and the driver, now restored to something akin to sanity, was taken to have his badly-bruised ankle attended to. Fortunately he was wearing a stout pair of boots, which had saved him from more serious injury.

We returned home, Rebel now in the sulks, walked into his kennel without so much as a backward glance at me.

The interview with the DI next morning was not a memory to cherish. As for 'the family', well, they broke into the woodyard at the other side of the city. Unfortunately, the woodyard 'paid out' on a Friday so the safe was empty. It was a bit of comfort to know they got it wrong as well.

CHAPTER 8

Resurrection

Quick change-over. Finish 10 p.m., return 5.45 a.m. Nobody liked it. It was 9.30 p.m. and I was trying to make my desk look less like the end of a paper chase and more like an efficient unit of administration – a daunting, if not impossible task. I was hoping for a quick finish. The phone rang; it was Eric in the front office.

'We have,' he said, 'a bit of a problem.' The fact that he described whatever it was as a 'bit of a problem' was no comfort. To Eric, everything short of murder was a 'bit of a problem'. Murder became 'a problem'.

'It's Paul [one of my probationers], Sarge, he would like you down at the flats – an old woman in trouble.'

All thoughts of a quick finish vanished. I picked up the keys to our second-hand Panda (the Inspectors had got a nice shiny new one and had kindly passed their old one down) and made my way to the flats. The concerned and curious were gathered around the entrance door. Why is it that the women always seemed to have their arms folded and the men their hands deep in their pockets – something to do with genes, perhaps?

Nellie, an attractive forty-something, who was said to be 'no better than she ought to be', but always appeared when any of her neighbours were in need of help, was to the fore.

'It's the old woman in the bottom flat, Sarge – we cannot make her hear.'

'Mind,' said her companion (who had very obviously never heard about or perhaps did not care about Weight Watchers) 'she hasn't been ower clivir for a bit.' My heart sank – I hated those jobs. Paul, who by this time must have been feeling a bit superfluous, finally got his two-pennyworth in.

'There's a side window, Sarge.' We went around the side, followed by the watchers, whose number had been enhanced as the club emptied.

'Give us a bunk up, Paul.' I balanced precariously on the window sill. There was a slight parting in the curtains and I peered through.

She was slumped down in the chair, a little dot of a thing, her right arm dangling slackly over the chair arm. I had seen it all before; nevertheless, I knocked on the window, just in case. There was no response: I hadn't expected any.

I took out my truncheon and gave a short, hard tap just above the window catch. Now when they do this on TV (you must have seen it) a neat, round hole appears, through which the super-efficient TV policeman carefully inserts his hand. Unfortunately I have never done it on TV and neither had that window. There was a loud shattering noise and the whole of the upper pane disintegrated and showered down upon those below, mainly Paul, who was still holding on to my legs. I made a mental note to have a word with him later. He knew my views on the use of strong language, especially in the presence of ladies, although, to be fair to the lad, most of the ladies present could have given him lessons.

The little figure in the chair did not move. I opened the window and climbed through onto the sideboard and from there to the floor, then walked quietly towards the chair – why is it, I wonder, we are so carefully quiet when we know we cannot be heard. I took hold of her wrist in a forlorn attempt to find a pulse (that's something else that always looks easy on TV). The little figure jerked erect and let out a piercing scream that would have awakened the real dead. I leapt back two yards, searched frantically for my own heart beat and started to babble rather incoherently,

'It's the police, it's the police,' and at the same time, pointing frantically at my chest – a 'me Tarzan' sort of gesture.

'What are you deein?' As she spoke, her eyes alighted on the window. 'Have yea broken me winder?'

'I couldn't open the door.'

'Ah know that, I had the bolts in.' I'd had enough; I unbolted the door and retreated into the street. Paul, a quick learner, stood aside to let Nellie into the house. I activated my radio:

'Eric, get the council to send the emergency repair van – broken window to board up.' He arrived half an hour later, looked at the window and said, 'B****y vandals.' Nellie appeared at the door.

'Never worry, Sarge, I'll clean up the mess.' I threw Paul the keys. 'You'd better drive.'

It was two weeks later, 9.40 p.m., reporting in for night shift.

Wally, who I was relieving, looked more like a rosy-cheeked farmer than a police officer. He welcomed me with a beaming smile. I knew immediately there was trouble.

'Just in time,' he said. 'I was going down to the flats – some old woman is in trouble.'

'I've had enough of that one, Wally.' The story of my escapade had gone around the division.

'No, no, its straight, it's just come in.' I shouted for Paul – at least he would know the way there. The folded arms and pocketed hands were in place. Nellie pushed a small, grey man towards us.

'It's her brother, Sarge, he calls a couple of nights a week on his way from the club.

'That's right, Sarge' – as if I would ever doubt Nellie. 'He's been banging at the door for a good quarter of an hour.'

'That's right, Sarge.'

'She had the doctor yesterday.' (This from Nellie's companion, who obviously still had not joined.) They were already heading for the window.

'Give us a bunk up, Paul.' The crack in the curtain wasn't quite as wide but I managed by screwing my neck at an excruciating angle to look through the window. The picture was somewhat different – the little figure was, on this occasion, slumped right forward, her head between her knees, both arms hanging down in front of her. I'd seen that posture before. I knocked loud and long on the window. On the previous occasion there was a little hope but this time I had none. Unfortunately, I was right. I reached for my truncheon. I heard an explosive exclamation from below and made a mental note to have a word with Paul – he well knew my opinion about taking God's name in vain.

This time, the blow was even shorter and harder; the result, however, entirely predictable. I climbed through and this time I did not need to take her pulse. I was still about two yards from her when her head came up and her scream rocked the walls. I froze in my tracks. I couldn't take much more of this sort of thing. Her eyes focussed and a look of disbelief came over her face.

'It's yea again.' I did not know what to say. 'Yes' seemed a little inadequate. Her glance went over my shoulder, a look of absolute incredulity in her eyes.

'You've broken me winder again.' I headed for the door.

'Never mind, Sarge – not your fault.' This from Nellie as she passed me going in. The little grey man followed her,

'Ah wish she would wear her hearing aid.'

'HEARING AID!'

'Aye, that's right, Sarge – can't hear a thing if you're not standing on top of her.' I turned on Paul (most unjustly).

'Did you not think after you had been told people had been banging on the door, to ask about her hearing?'

'No, Sarge.' And then, gazing over my shoulder at no one or nowhere in particular.

'Nobody else did either; shall I get the emergency repair man?' Discretion being the better part of valour, I retreated to the Panda.

A few days later, the Superintendent, who had a waspish sense of humour, said, 'We are quite proud of you, Sarge, even your friend Jesus [my faith was never a secret] only brought them back from the dead the once.' This was, I thought, a little unfair – after all, my little old lady was not really dead. On the other hand, I hope I will not be thought to be irreverent when I say that our Lord did have an advantage over me – he knew Lazarus was hard of hearing.

Perhaps you would care to look it up: John 11, verse 43: 'He cried with a **loud** voice "Lazarus, come out".'

I wish I had known about my Lazarus.

CHAPTER 9

Mrs Constance Olivia Murray

I CONFESS THAT I HAVE NO recollection of this lady at all. Whether she was fat, thin, tall or short, I remember not. I came across her whilst browsing through an old pocket book: 22 February 1957 and if you want to be precise, it was 10.30 a.m. Having read her name, I felt compelled to read on – it has, I think you will agree, a certain ring to it: Mrs Constance Olivia Murray. One can picture the dear lady serving tea on the lawn, or presiding on the Magistrates' Bench; perhaps President of the Town Ladies' Guild, or Women's Institute.

Alas, she was none of these – no lawn surrounded her home; she lived at 33 Millbank Road, a row of Victorian terrace houses going into genteel decline. Her chief claim to fame was that she owned a black and white terrier dog without having a licence for same. For in those far-off days, you had to have a licence to keep a dog. It cost (if memory serves me right) 7s 6d – seven shillings and six pence and no, I do not know the present-day equivalent. Each quarter of the year we received from the local council office a list of all those people who had taken out a licence in the same quarter of the previous year but had failed to renew it. We then trooped around the town knocking on doors, enquiring why the licence had not been renewed. The number of deaths in the dog population rose alarmingly each quarter – tearful owners would tell us how much they missed their pet. If we happened to hear a faint bark or doggy snuffle in the background, we did not, as they do on the 'telly', kick the door down and rush in but put it down to a haunted kennel and carried on. There were, I must confess, those occasions when we killed poor Fido ourselves. Well, after you had walked across town three times in all sorts of weather and on each occasion found no-one at home, you got a bit fed up and wrote 'dog dead', at the same time offering up a silent prayer that it would not arise before resurrection day and bite one of the neighbours.

Just who compiled those lists I never knew or how indeed they went about it. No computers those days – just large ledgers with pen and ink or copying ink pencils. I often wonder if the task was given to a new starter to get him used to office work, or to someone having grown old in the service of the council, as a gentle wind-down to retirement. I am inclined towards the latter. I can see him (the chances of it being a 'her' in those days were fairly slight) sitting in the office with its green-painted walls. All the council and police offices, with the exception of Chief Executive's and Superintendent's, were painted the same dreadful colour. It was rumoured that the works department had bought a job lot at an ex-WD sale. There our hero would sit with, on his left hand, last year's list and on his right, the current one. What did he do, I wonder, when he found someone who had failed to renew a licence? Did he, as footballers do when they have scored a goal (which, after all, is what they are paid for) leap into the air then throw himself to the floor and slide along the brown office lino? The way the cleaners used to buff it, his speed would be such that he would be in danger of crashing through the wall. Did he, I wonder, do again as footballers do and dash round hugging and kissing everyone? I think not – kissing in public was not the 'done thing' in those days, especially in council offices. The only public kissing was at the end of a marriage ceremony, when the vicar would solemnly inform the bridegroom that, 'You may now kiss the bride.' I have no doubt that he had kissed her a few times before but this being possibly read by youngsters, we will draw a veil over such matters. I am sure he would merely quietly dip his pen in the inkwell (only Heads of Departments and Superintendents could afford fountain pens) and quietly place a tick against the offending name.

The reason Mrs Constance Olivia Murray had not a licence, she said, was that 'I am on "The Parish".' The nearest present-day equivalent I can give our younger readers is 'Income Support' or 'Non-Contributory Job Seeker's Allowance', paid out by the Benefits Agency. That's progress for you. I told her I would call back the following day, Monday 25 February: 11.45 a.m., when I again spoke to the lady. She still had no licence because the Public Assistance (posh speech for 'The Parish') had not paid her money. In the best traditions of diplomacy when faced with an impasse, I extended the deadline. I have no doubt you are thinking what a lovely kind policeman I was – the truth is somewhat different. I just could not think that one poor little black and white terrier, whose mistress was on 'The Parish', was worth the trouble of, first, a written report (joined-up writing, no typewriter) then a summons, followed by Court. It seemed a rather big hammer to crack such a small nut.

Tuesday 26 February, 11.15 a.m., 33 Millbank Road. Mrs Constance Olivia Murray produced to me Dog Licence No. JH053109, issued at 2.15pm on 25th February.

Hurrah for 'The Parish'.

CHAPTER 10

Early Days

NONE OF THE HOSTEL RESIDENTS LIKED early days (6 a.m. to 2 p.m.) It was not the shift itself but the constant fear of sleeping in. In later years there was a wifely elbow to ease you out of bed but then you were on your own. Ben slept in three times and was sent to see the Superintendent, a kindly man never known to raise his voice in anger. Why, he wondered, did Ben sleep in so often. Ben said he simply could not get used to the shift. The Superintendent thought awhile then said he would have a word with the Inspector and arrange for Ben to have a month of early days to familiarise himself with the shift. If he would like an extension he only had to ask. He left shortly after that (Ben not the Superintendent) to do something for the BBC. I'm sure it would not be the early disc jockey slot.

Tom and I shared a room and relied on an ancient travelling alarm clock; inevitably it let us down. We arrived at the station out of breath having run the two miles from the hostel in full uniform. We were not allowed to travel in civvies, you were on duty from the moment you stepped out of the house, no one had cars so we travelled by bus, bike or on foot which meant a constant presence of police officers on the street. Modern Chief Constables should take note. The Sergeant gazed up at the office clock which showed a quarter past the hour. Had we, he enquired, slept in? Having received an answer in the affirmative, he said not to worry. We should go back to the hostel and get our sleep then come in for two till ten. Not forgetting of course that we would be back on early the following morning. What I wonder would the present day young officer say. We merely turned around and went back to the hostel.

It was the following morning and I was making my way to the pillar for my eight o'clock point when the pillar gong started to sound. I hurried forward and picked up the phone. It was Geoff in the Town Office. A 999 call – a woman frightened of her husband and wanting him out of the house. This was the sort of call you expected at 8 p.m. not 8 a.m. I made my way towards the address in a nearby street. No need to look for the address, she was standing in the doorway. There was only one word to describe her – huge – in every way. She had the build of an all-in-heavyweight wrestler. Massive arms folded across a chest that had long since gone from impressive to intimidating. As I approached she flung out her arm with a Shakespearean gesture pointing into the house.

'Ah want him out. He's me second and Ah wish Ah had never seen him,' she said.

'Where is he?' I asked.

'Up there,' she said, pointing to the stairs at the end of the passage. I approached with some trepidation. What sort of monster was he that this woman was afraid of. There were three doors at the top of the stairs, two tight shut one slightly open, I could hear a faint noise coming from it. I stretched my arm to its fullest extent and pushed it open. He was sat on the bed, a little rotund figure, his right hand caressing a cheek that was turning a bright red.

'What happened?' I asked.

'She hit me with this.' He lifted up a Smith's alarm clock from the bed. Large white face, distinctive black numbers, three legs and two bells on the top.

'She wants you out,' I said.

'Ah want to get out but Ah'm not going down there while she is in the door.' He bent down and picked up a battered old suitcase. I sympathised with him.

'Wait here,' I said. I went down stairs.

'You will have to go into the living-room,' I told her.

'No one tells me where to go in my own house,' came the reply. I lost patience.

'Either you go into the living-room or I am going and you can sort it out yourself!' I said. The chest began to heave and tremble, an awesome sight. I stood my ground with some trepidation. Suddenly she turned, marched through the door and clashed it behind her. He scuttled down the stairs like a frightened rabbit. I followed him out.

'Where will you go?'

'My brother lives down the town.'

'Oh, right.' I watched him set off down the street, case in hand. He was leaning to the left to keep it off the ground, his little legs working overtime.

At the end of the shift I called at the Co-op and bought one of those Smith's alarm clocks. I never slept in again.

CHAPTER 11

Killer Bates

THERE WERE ONLY THREE OCCASIONS in my service when I was called upon to deal with incidents involving firearms, that is, if you do not count youths with air rifles and the odd poacher with a double-barrelled shotgun neither of which ever gave me the slightest cause for concern. On this occasion I was walking down the main street through my village. I say 'my village' because that is how we viewed our 'patch'. When you were given a detached beat, your very own area to be responsible for twenty-four hours a day seven days a week (rest days were never sacrosanct) it was considered something of a promotion. We took great pride in our patch and over the years developed affection for the people – well nearly all of them, there was always the odd exception. The Superintendent would occasionally pop out to have a chat but we were mostly left on our own, under the eye of the Section Sergeant, to look after things. It was 11.30 on a Friday night and I was heading for the club.

Friday night was dance night and there was always a full house. There was rarely any trouble, they had a good committee, which had a few, carefully selected, big lads on it. The sight of a Panda racing up the street with blue light flashing shattered my peace. I stepped to the edge of the pavement where I could be seen. The Panda pulled up beside me and the driver wound the window down. Both he and his companion were very much younger in years and service than myself. They were both obviously relieved to see me. This faith which our younger officers placed in the 'Detached Beat' men was at times rather worrying, as upon this occasion.

'It's a three nine call, Ray. Somebody called 'Killer Bates' shooting a gun outside the old people's bungalows' I opened the back door and clambered in.

'It's your first right and second left then about half way up the street on your left,' and I added swiftly as the driver started to somewhat enthusiastically rev the engine, 'take it easy I'm a married man with children.'

34

I never discovered why he had the nickname 'Killer' apart from the fact that he used to be a member of a boxing booth on the fairground. The only ones in the street were Bob and Jack: Bob, a widower and Jack, a feisty Jack Russell terrier which was his constant companion. First things first. I bent down to scratch Jack's ears. It pays to be friends with feisty Jack Russells, ask any postman or paper-lad. I spoke to Bob,

'What's this about Killer shooting folk?'

'It's nowt to worry thee sell about, Ray,' he replied. 'Their Harry, Killer's eighteen year old grandson, cracked Big Kenny out (another eighteen year old but a big lad who had the reputation of being able 'to handle himself') at the dance and Kenny gave him a hiding. Killer must have been vexed and decided to give Kenny a fright. Anyway as I was coming out with Jack, Kenny came up the street. Killer must have been watching for him because just as Kenny walked past he came out with his gun, shouted at Kenny and fired it into the air.'

'What,' I asked, 'did Kenny do?'

'He called him a stupid old bugger and took off.'

'Are you sure he shot into the air?' I asked. Bob answered as if he could not believe the question.

'Why aye I'm sure you don't think he would shoot the lad.' I turned and went towards Killer's bungalow. The Panda crew, now thoroughly bemused followed. I stopped a moment.

'Tell the office,' I instructed, 'no further assistance required. I am with you. We will report to the office shortly.' I knocked on the door. It was answered by Mrs Bates, a gentle, grey-haired old lady.

'Come in, Mr Gibbon. I feel properly ashamed. I don't know what he is coming to.' 'He' was in his armchair next to the fire.

'What happened Harry?' (I always gave him his baptismal name.)

'Kenny gave our Harry a hiding tonight although I suppose it was partly Harry's fault but Kenny is getting too cocky so I thought I would give him a fright, bring him down a peg.' I tried to look like a stern police officer.

'You had no right to shoot at him.' He looked at me indignantly.

'I didn't try to shoot him. I wouldn't do that just fired into the air to give him a fright.'

'Where's the gun?' He got out of the chair and went through the back returning with a small bore shotgun – they were often referred to as 'garden guns', and a small box containing cartridges. The gun was obviously well cared for.

'Who,' I asked, 'has been using this?'

'Our Harry takes it up the allotments and sometimes down the river to shoot rats.' I was getting annoyed about this gun. Why had I not known of its existence and Harry's use of it? I turned to go.

'I don't suppose you have such a thing as a licence?'

'Didn't think about it, Ray.' I had one final try.

'How long have you had it?' He looked puzzled and his brow furrowed as he concentrated on the question. I gave up, I turned to Mrs Bates.

'No need to keep you up any longer, I'll call in the morning.'

We paid a visit to Ken. His father answered the door.

'Hullo Ray – anything wrong?'

'Nothing to worry about,' I said. 'I would like a word with Kenny.' I was invited in, Kenny was reading the sports paper.

'Ray wants a word with you,' said his father nodding at Kenny. Kenny got to his feet, with a 'Hullo PC Gibbon.' There were certain standards to be observed by the younger members and Kenny was aware of it; if he had forgotten his father would have swiftly reminded him.

'You are not in any trouble Kenny,' I assured him, 'just tell me what happened.' His story tallied with what I had already heard.

'Do you want to make any complaint about it?' I asked.

'You mean like report him to you, PC Gibbon?' His tone was one of amazement.

'That's right, Kenny.'

'Why no. I'll probably get him a pint in tomorrow night.'

'Are you at work in the morning?' I asked.

'No, PC Gibbon.'

'My office then at ten o'clock, I will need a statement.' We left; my two young colleagues were obviously trying to fit all this in with training school lessons and finding it difficult.

At the office I found that the Chief Inspector, a man of great experience who was not only held in respect but also affection, was ensconced in the office chair with a cigarette in his hand and a pot of tea at his elbow. It was his wont on a Friday and Saturday night to have a couple of pints in the club then hold court in the office until the early hours when he would go home – he lived next door to the office – to bed. He gave me a broad smile.

'What's this, Gibbon lad, people running about on your patch with guns?' I gave him my story. He took a pull on his cigarette.

'What,' he asked, 'are we doing about it?'

'I thought, Sir,' I said, 'about a gun but no licence.'

'I think,' he said thoughtfully, 'the Superintendent will want a bit more than that.' We both knew that he and the Superintendent were old friends who rarely disagreed.

'How about,' he added, 'discharging a gun within 50 feet of the highway as well, then in view of his previous good character, you ask for a caution. I presume he has previous good character?' I assured him that a newborn babe could hardly be less blameless.

'You lads,' he said nodding at the Panda crew, 'had better get on protecting the public.' It was said with a smile. They left suitably impressed if still somewhat bemused. He nodded towards the teapot.

'Get yourself a pot of tea while Tom –' he nodded towards the Town Office man – 'sorts that gun out.' Tom had served with the Chief Inspector in many places over many years so was privileged.

What I wonder would happen today if a similar message was received, armed units with flashing lights and sirens, the street sealed off and Killer invited, over a megaphone, to come out with his hands on his head, I do not say this with any sense of mockery or criticism. I recognise that I had a distinct advantage over my successors of today. I was a member of that proud race, 'the detached beat man'. I appreciate that we now live in a different society. A young constable and his wife may not look upon being given their own area to look after twenty-four hours a day and sometimes seven days a week without extra pay, as not only a promotion but also a privilege. However I cannot help thinking they are missing a great deal. It had great rewards.

I did not go after Killer without back up because I was brave or possessed of great courage. I went in because I knew Killer was eighty years old, had a limp, walked with a stick and was half blind – and of course I had Bob's assurance that there was 'Nowt to worry thee sell about.' I knew exactly what danger I was in.

CHAPTER 12

The Ambulance Man

'THE AMBULANCE SERVICE,' said the Superintendent, 'are going on strike and we have to provide emergency cover. I am putting you in charge, Sergeant.' (How very kind I thought)

'You will need four men' (he had great respect for his women officers just could not think of a word that incorporated men and women), 'working twelve-hour shifts, preferably with a knowledge of first aid, and a suitable vehicle equipped as well as you can.' There would, I thought, be no shortage of volunteers, all that overtime for sitting around the office.

'I have a good contact in the St John Ambulance, Sir.' He smiled.

'I have been down that road Sergeant. It is forbidden.' He reached for his pen and turned to his paperwork. 'Let me know by lunch-time how you get on.' It was 10 a.m., not much time to create an ambulance service out of my motley crew. On the way to my office I poked my head into the front office. I spoke to Eric, my office man, noted for his ability to do miracles.

'Contact everyone on duty in the Sub-Div. and find out who has any first aid qualifications. You have an hour.' Eric, noted for his calm under fire merely nodded. I found Les and George, our civvy employees, worth their weight in gold, having their ten o'clock cuppa. I wanted, I said, the divvy van converted into an ambulance, scrubbed out and disinfected and equipped with a stretcher. They never even blinked.

'There is,' said George, 'a stretcher in the back of the garage.' We adjourned to the garage where George produced from a distant and dark corner a stretcher from the Second World War era. It consisted of two poles with canvas stretched between them and mounted on four iron legs. It was covered with a thick layer of dust. I explained my problem.

'Leave it with us, Sarge,' they said and I did. By lunchtime they produced a gleaming clean van and stretcher, both reeking of disinfectant. Eric had identified four potential ambulance crew, Bob,

Paul, Jim and Steve. Paul had been a nurse, Bob had his life-saving medal. He could, explained Eric, do artificial respiration. The other two had some vague connection with first aid. I called them into the office and informed them of the duties they had just volunteered for. I informed the Superintendent and invited him to inspect my ambulance and crew. He declined, politely, obviously he had every faith in me or just did not wish to get involved.

The strike began. Two days later we had our first emergency call late in the evening. I was on two-ten shift so decided to go along. The call was to a block of flats, the sixth floor. An elderly man had collapsed. We arrived, Bob, Paul and myself complete with stretcher, to find a very distressed elderly lady with her husband on the floor. It was obvious even to our inexperienced eyes that he had had a stroke. She had, she said, sent for the emergency doctor service over an hour ago and no one had responded so she had rung 999. He was semi-conscious and obviously in need of expert medical attention. We placed him carefully on the stretcher and carried him to the lift. It was only when the lift arrived that I realised that the stretcher would not go in. Bob came to the rescue.

'There are doors at the back, Sarge, that open up.' He went to the back of the lift and opened up two doors. They went the full width of the lift but only half the height creating a dark box like effect. We started to put the stretcher in.

'Sarge, Sarge,' again from Bob, a very observant lad, 'turn him around.'

'What for, Bob?'

'If you put him in head first and he comes around he will think we have buried him.' The stretcher was swiftly reversed. Eventually we arrived at the ground floor, removed our patient from the lift and placed him in the van. A World War Two battlefield stretcher placed on the floor of a commercial van is not the best way of transporting an elderly man who had suffered a stroke. I asked Bob to drive carefully whilst Paul and I knelt by the stretcher. I slid my arms under his head and shoulders whilst Paul slid his beneath his hips and knees to try and absorb the bumps.

We arrived at the hospital to be welcomed by a doctor and nurse, alerted by Eric. The doctor's 'Oh God,' when he viewed the interior of the 'ambulance' said it all.

'Very gently, please.'

'Right, doctor.' We carefully lifted our patient and carried him into the casualty department and placed the stretcher gently on the floor. Two porters, more unsung heroes, carefully instructed us in the art of lifting our patient from the low stretcher onto a bed without killing him.

Some two weeks later, the strike thankfully over, I was again in the Superintendent's office. He handed me a letter, neatly written. It was from our patient's wife. Thanks, she said, to the kindness of the police officers, her husband had made a good recovery and had returned home. (Eric wondered if she had meant 'despite'). She enclosed a ten shilling note, which would leave a hole in their pension, for 'Police Funds'.

'Copy of the letter on the notice board, Sergeant, Paul and Bob to deliver the receipt and see they are all right.' I dispatched them on their errand. It took much longer than it should have done. It was, they said due to the cups of tea and chocolate biscuits it would have been churlish to refuse. I suspected they became fairly regular visitors after that. I never objected, the Superintendent was very keen on what he called keeping in touch with the public.

CHAPTER 13

Him

AT 4.30 SUNDAY MORNING THERE was a fine misty rain failing. Eric and I were clearing the cells of our overnight visitors. We had three, all D and D. We had dispatched the first two, both in their late teens – more stupid than criminal. As they left Eric told them in his most avuncular manner that the walk home would do them good, it was a good three miles to where they lived. Eric nodded in the direction of the cells.

'Do you want him out, Sarge?' The contempt in his voice was ill-concealed, it was if he could not bear to give the man a name. Unusual for Eric who was normally never one to hold a grudge.

'Yes, wheel him out, Eric.' Eric disappeared into the cellblock and brought 'him' out and placed him behind the counter in the charge office.

'Will you need me, Sarge?' he asked in the tone of voice that indicated he hoped I would not. It was if he did not wish to be in the same room. I looked at our prisoner, a bent old man and wondered how anyone could deteriorate so quickly.

'No, Eric, you can go back to the office.' Tom and Bill had brought him in. Tom, just out of probation, Bill, with a year to go. Neither of them knew anything about him. Tom had explained:

'He was having words with a bunch of young lads, Sarge. We told him to go away but he would not go. We brought him in, we thought if we left him with them he would be a hospital case.' I began to muse upon the thought that those who had known him better would have left him to his fate. I began to wonder what I would have done had I been there then decided I did not want to go down that road. In his day he had been an infamous 'hard man'. He had no sense of loyalty and less of pity or mercy. He hired out his large knuckled fists, hard muscular body and expertise with the pickaxe handle to the highest bidder. The body controlled by a mind that enjoyed inflicting pain. I had heard him described as 'pure evil.' He would take your money to 'sort out' your opponents and then

41

take a higher bid from someone else to 'sort out' you. He was hated and feared even amongst his own. I was brought out of my reverie by his voice.

'Could I have a smoke, Sarge?' The voice was low and rather husky, gone was the old mocking arrogance. I emptied his property bag onto the counter and pushed the 'makings' over to him. He rolled the cigarette with the economy of tobacco that was the sure mark of those who had spent time behind bars. The deftness had gone, his movements were slow as he concentrated on an action that a short time ago would have been automatic.

Whilst he was occupied I took a moment to have a good look at him. I knew that despite his appearance he was only in his late fifties, the thick brown hair had gone to a thin wispy grey, and the large knuckled hands were thin and criss-crossed with thin blue, almost transparent, veins. Purple patches covered his cheekbones. The powerful shoulders rounded. Whether his swift decline was due to his life-style or to some disease that was ravaging his body I neither knew nor, to be honest, cared. On those occasions when we tangled with him we always went mob-handed and there were always bruises to be nursed afterwards. I recalled the night he had wrenched the cell toilet out of the floor and smashed it to smithereens. Seeing him now, to be honest, brought a sense of relief. He sucked on his cigarette with the appetite of the true addict. I pushed the rest of his property over to him, a few shillings. I remembered the day when there would have been a large roll of 'tenners'. He picked up the pen and without any prompting signed the charge sheet. I turned to put the property bag back into the cupboard. When I turned back he was standing by the door. I nodded and he made his way up the passage and to the office door. I watched him as he walked slowly with bowed shoulders out onto the road, no longer feared just hated.

It was an hour later when I was preparing to go off duty that I realised that the cell keys were missing. I had last seen them on the charge office counter when I was dealing with him. I remembered him standing by the door as I turned from the property cupboard. I had a word with the Inspector. He advised that I take one of the lads with me when I went to get him. I decided to wait an hour and then give Ron a ring. Ron was our senior DC – he and I had collected our good conduct medals together the previous week. Ron had known him and had been dealing with him for a number of years. I explained what had happened and my suspicions.

'I'll go now, Ray. Put one of the lads at the end of the street although I do not think there will be any trouble with him now.' An hour later Ron came in to my office and dropped the keys on my desk.

'You are not going to believe this,' he said. 'He saw me through the curtains and came straight out with the keys and said he was sorry because you had always been straight he did not know why he had done it.' He paused a moment then said, 'I think I know why he did it, he had to prove something to himself and let you know that you still could not turn your back on him.' I put my report on the Superintendent's desk then went home to bed.

It was late afternoon when the phone rang. It was the Chief Inspector.

'Had your sleep out, Ray?'

'Yes, Bob' – we had known each other for a long time.

'Superintendent would like a word with you.'

'I thought he would, Bob, give me an hour.' As I walked into the sanctum the Superintendent pushed my report across his desk. It was obvious from his attitude and tone that he was not best pleased.

'A man is arrested, especially him, and whilst at my station commits a theft and you tell me that he has been cautioned by a DC and recommend no further action. What is it, Sarge? Frightened? It gets out and we are a laughing stock.' I waited a while, I was not quite sure how to put my thoughts and feelings into words.

'No, Sir, it's not that it's because he is just not worth the bother, he is not that important he just doesn't matter any more and the sooner he knows it the better.' The Superintendent leaned back into his chair, a slightly shocked look on his face.

'That's a bit harsh, Sarge, especially from you, I would hate to think that I did not matter to anyone anymore.' Silence, as they say, reigned for a while, then he spoke again.

'All right, Sarge, I'll think about it.'

I never heard from the Superintendent again on that subject. I never heard of 'him' again either. That is well over thirty years ago now and I have no doubt he is no longer with us. As I look back I realise that I never heard of a wife or family, certainly he never had what you would call real friends, everyone was too frightened of him for true friendship to exist. They say we mellow, as we grow older. I don't know if that is true but as I look back I think the Superintendent was right and I was 'a bit harsh'. It must be a particular sort of hell where you do not matter to anyone. I remember that I have wept over dogs. As I said it was a long time ago and now I find myself hoping that when he went there was someone somewhere who, for whatever reason, shed a tear over him.

CHAPTER 14

The Charmer

IT WAS 8 A.M. ON A CRISP, COLD, winter morning. There had been snow through the night the roads and footpaths were still showing a white coat. It was Sunday, usually quiet and an ideal time to clear up the paperwork; I was working my way steadily through a pile of brown folders on my desk. The phone rang, it was Eric.

'Bob's been on, Sarge, he's found the Jag that was stolen from the hotel across the town. He's on his way in, I'm ringing the hotel to speak to the owner.' I felt a warm glow, what a good start to the day.

'That's great, Eric, keep me informed.' I returned to the folders with a lighter heart. It was some twenty minutes later when the phone rang again. Again it was Eric, as soon as he spoke I knew there was trouble. Whenever Eric had to report that a clanger had been dropped he dropped his voice an octave. It was as if he was preparing you for what was to come. He sounded as if he was talking to a potential suicide, asking them to step back from the cliff edge. Things he appeared to be saying were not really that bad.

'It's about the car, Sarge.'

'What about it Eric?'

'Well I rang the hotel but the owner had already left for the station, I rang the British Transport lads at the station, they said the train had left but it was stopping at Durham. They would get someone to board the train and see if the owner wanted to come back for his car, he would only have to wait about ten minutes for a return train.' There was a pause and I tightened my grip on the phone.

'Carry on, Eric.'

'Well Sarge,' Eric's voice was descending to a whisper, 'that was when Bob came in and said the car doors had been left open and there was snow all over the interior.' Relief swept over me. That was bad but not insurmountable; we should, with a concerted effort, soon clean it up if the owner did appear which he was highly unlikely to. I realised Eric was still speaking.

'And the wheels are all missing, Sarge.' There was a time some years earlier when I had walked into a low wooden beam as my head hit the beam the world seemed to come to an end and I was plunged into darkness. I was incapable of either speech or movement, there was no beam about on this occasion but the effect was much the same. I took a deep breath and steeled myself to ask the next question.

'Where is the owner, Eric?' The reply was a little while in coming as if Eric was finding the answer difficult; finally it came.

'He's on his way back to Newcastle, Sarge, I've asked the traffic lads to bring them here.'

'Just what' – I realised my voice was rising to a crescendo so stopped and started again. I tried, like Eric, to drop my voice an octave.

'Just what do you intend to do with them when they get here, provide them with a special train?' Eric's voice oozed over the phone.

'I'm working on that, Sarge.' I put the phone down. I remembered it was Sunday when trains were cancelled all over the country so 'essential' work could be carried out. Just what, I wondered, would I say to the Superintendent on Monday, or say to the Superintendent 'Complaints and Discipline'? Could I, I wondered, fake a heart attack get rushed off to hospital then apply for medical retirement? I was still thinking when the traffic car arrived. I peered around the curtain of my window. Bob and Eric were assisting an elderly man and two women out of the car and conducting them into the office while the traffic lads trotted behind with cases. They came down the passage, I buried my head in the brown folders, as they went into the police club. I waited for Eric to summon me.

Ten minutes went by, nothing happened. I waited another five minutes then decided I really ought to do something. I walked into the club steeling myself for battle. There was an air of complete peace and calm. Eric, tea towel folded over his left arm, was pouring tea for the ladies into cups that were kept in the cupboard in the Superintendent's office for the use of himself and his visitors. The biscuits he was proffering obviously came from the same place. Bob was chatting to the man, making arrangements for the local Jaguar agent to collect the car. I approached the ladies and began to apologise for the inconvenience we had caused them. They smiled kindly at me and said there was no need to apologise. This officer –

1. Nigel, Rebel, Alison

2. Rebel

3. Author and Rebel looking for missing child

4. Ryton Village Fete 1977

5. Margaret and Author, retirement 1984

6. Mayor, 2003/2004

7. *Mayor's Bodyguard and Members of the City Council – see Appendix*

8 *Author and Margaret meeting Prince Andrew on board HMS Invincible*

9. Sir Paul Nicholson, receiving Freeman of the City

10. *Author's eightieth birthday 2009*

they gazed upon Eric with something akin to affection – was looking after them very well and had even arranged another train for them which went by a route they much preferred. I was obviously viewed as being surplus to requirements, not I reflected, an unusual situation where Eric was concerned. I bestowed a look upon Eric which informed him that if he did not wish to come to a sticky end he had better speak to me in my office and left. He appeared a few minutes later accompanied by a beaming smile.

'Bit of luck there, Sarge, I gave the B.T. lads a ring whilst this lot were on their way from Durham and they found another train for where they want to go.' He glanced at his watch. 'It leaves in three quarters of an hour, I'll have to get them moving.' He disappeared. He appeared in my office some fifteen minutes later with a large mug.

'Cup of tea, Sarge.'

'Thanks, Eric, our guests left all right?'

'Why of course, Sarge.' I had a word with the traffic lads at bait time. Our guests, they said, had been met at the station by a B.T. Sergeant, and two porters then escorted them to the train like royalty and placed them in a first-class compartment. I had a word with the Superintendent on Monday morning – better me than someone else – I kept names and personalities out as far as possible. The word 'we' was mainly used. He gave me a brief lecture on the advisability of checking my facts before making decisions and let me go. I was back in his office a week later, he handed me a letter it had come to him via the Chief Constable's Office.

'Have a read of that, Sergeant.' It was from the wife of the Jaguar owner. She wished, she wrote, to bring to the Chief Constable's notice the efficiency and kindness of the officers who had dealt with the theft of their car. She wished in particular to thank the charming officer who had cared for them at the police station and arranged their train home.

'Let Eric have sight of it sign it then return it to me.' I headed for the door; the Superintendent spoke again.

'You and Eric have been together for some time, Sergeant, how would you feel about exchanging him with another shift?' I thought for a moment of a life without Eric and his 'cup of tea, Sarge' in moments of stress and his innate ability to bring us out of all sorts of situations 'smelling of roses'. It was not to be thought of.

'I think, Sir,' I said, 'Eric is best with me.' He smiled.

'I think you are right, Sergeant.' So it remained to the night of my retirement when at the end of the night he saw me out of the door and to my car.

'Take care, Ray.'

'Take care, Eric.'

CHAPTER 15

Team Work

I READ THE OTHER THE DAY of the problems 'Chiefy' is having with manpower and money. He will be relieved to know that I have the answer to his problems. He must return to the day of the 'twenty-four hour detached beat officer'. I doubt if any young couple today would be willing to be tied down twenty-four hours a day, rest days excepted although they ran from midnight to midnight. In those somewhat far-off days it was considered an honour to be sent to a detached beat. Your house was on your patch with its adjoining office from which you ruled your area. Even the Div. Super. thought twice about interfering with you as long as you had things under control. Your wife was considered as much a part of the force as you were. When the locals knocked on the door and you were out they expected your wife to deal with their problem. Panic-stricken farmers knocking on the office door: 'The wagon's here for the pigs and I have forgotten to get the licence.' If I was out Margaret would fill out the movement licence and forge my signature. On my next visit to the farm there would usually be a paper bag with half a dozen eggs in it popped in my pocket. Have you ever tried riding a motor cycle with half a dozen eggs in your pocket without breaking any? It ought to be a compulsory test.

There was one occasion when Margaret cradled a dying man in her arms on the office floor whilst I tried vainly to resuscitate him. That is another story.

This one started at 1 a.m. on a bitter cold Sunday morning. We were weekend off (Saturday and Sunday every six weeks); we were woken by a persistent knocking at the office door plus the barking of Flash, our collie dog. I opened the door to an icy blast. Bill and Harry, two of our locals, were supporting a young lad with blood streaming from his face. Another young man hovered in the background.

'Bring him in lads.' They brought him in and lowered him onto a chair. As they did so Harry told me,

'He skidded on the bend, Ray, and hit the lamp post, the roads are b****y treacherous.' By this time Margaret had appeared, disappeared and reappeared with a washing up bowl which she thrust into Bill's hands instructing him to 'hold it under his face'. She disappeared again. I reflected that it was a bit late to save his suit, already blood-soaked; in those days young men wore a suit when they went out on the town on Saturday night. The girls kept their underwear undercover. Margaret reappeared with towels snatched from the airing cupboard, and a bowl of water and began to sponge the young man's face to assess the damage, broken nose, cut lips and mashed up mouth, no seat belts in those days. I sent for the ambulance, and then got a few particulars from the other young man. The injured one lived with his parents a few miles along the road. I knew of them vaguely. They lived in a large detached house, his father was the owner of a small chain of chemists shops.

Bill and Harry were both in their early fifties and worked at the local colliery. I did not ask them what they were doing out in the early hours of the morning. I knew they were both (very) slightly inebriated. There had been (without doubt) a lock in at 'The Bull'. Bar lights only, tight drawn curtains and muted conversation. O Happy Days. This twenty-four hour drinking has destroyed all the pleasure.

The ambulance arrived, the driver voicing Harry's opinion that the roads were b****y treacherous. The ambulance left, his friend with no hope of any taxi or other transport was put to bed in the spare room. If you think this was somewhat reckless I should tell you that Flash slept on the landing and was not to be argued with. Bill and Harry departed for their homes. I was not bothered about Harry, his wife was a jolly sort of person who would probably content herself with telling him to be quiet and get into bed. Bill's wife was a bit different, she ran the house on a strict set of rules, no boots beyond the kitchen, a cardboard box was kept just inside the back door for slippers, certain hours were to be observed. His homecoming, I thought, would be a trifle more difficult, although they both had a wonderful excuse.

We went to bed. We were woken at 7 a.m. by Nigel, our nine month old son. Our lodger joined us for breakfast. The local garage taxi man was contacted to collect our lodger and see to the car. By

10 a.m. we were getting back to normal. Margaret, sorting through a sinkful of bloodstained towels discovered she had used two of her best ones (hand embroidered, visitors only, she never did get the bloodstains out). We were getting ready to go to Margaret's mother for Sunday dinner (Yorkshire puddings to die for) when there was a knock at the office door. I opened it to an immaculately dressed elderly man; over his shoulder I caught a glimpse of a two-tone Humber Hawk. He had called, he said, to say thank you for caring for his son and to tell us he was not seriously injured. Could he have a word with my wife. I took him through to the living room. He shook Margaret's hand and repeated his thanks; after having a word with Nigel and Flash he left. I accompanied him to the door. As I turned to go back into the house Margaret came hurrying down the hall waving a white sealed envelope.

'He has left this on the table.' I took it from her and hurried out side to where our visitor was about to drive away. I started to say,

'This envelope . . .' when he held up his hand.

'That envelope, Mr Gibbon, is addressed to Mrs Gibbon, it has nothing to do with you or me, it is from my wife to her.' He smiled and drove away. The envelope contained £10 together with a note from the lad's mother thanking Margaret for caring for her son. The money was, she said, a little token of her gratitude. It was spent on two new towels (visitors for the use of) and a new steam iron, ours being on the blink. I made no mention of it in my accident report (I had to put one in as the lamp post was somewhat bent), after all it was nothing to do with me, and the one thing Margaret would not do was keep a pocket-book.

CHAPTER 16

A Sunny Sunday

IT WAS LATE AFTERNOON ON A beautiful summer's day; Sunday and the world seemed to be at peace. Geoff and I were having a ride around the (large) housing development being built on the outskirts of the town. We were trying to keep down the petty thieving that went on at weekends. Some of the worst culprits were the people who had bought the houses on the first phase. They would scurry around at nights and weekends with their B&Q wheelbarrows collecting bricks, paving stones sand etc. with which to make paths and patios. The site manager said he was not too bothered about them as the firm put £250 on the price of each house to cover for such eventualities. The DI said he did not care what was on the houses, he had his crime figures to think about. We were looking at a large four-bedroomed detached house on the outskirts of the development. It was (according to the sales blurb) a 'spacious superior detached house with, amongst other things, spacious reception rooms, four bedrooms, two en suite, detached double garage with grassed paddock to rear.' All for £95,000. Who, we wondered, could afford that sort of money for a house. The radio crackled into life. It was Eric, a report of sound of shots coming from Mill House Farm. It was only a mile or so up the road so we were quickly on the scene. It had the tired worn look of old properties that have been neglected. The front door was wide open; there was no reply to our knock so we made our way, carefully, inside. We went into the living room, it was sparsely furnished, two small armchairs, a sofa, table with four chairs and the inevitable long sideboard that could always be found in any farm living-room.

An elderly grey-haired man sat in one of the chairs staring into the dying embers of the fire. There was a stillness about him that was disconcerting. I spoke.

'Hello there, are you all right?' He turned his head slowly towards me and said,

'Aye,' then returned his gaze to the fire. Geoff had a go.

'We were told there were shots being fired.' This time he did not take his eyes from the fire but simply said,

'He's upstairs.' There was an air of hopelessness about him, it was if life had dealt him a hand he was totally incapable of playing and whatever had happened upstairs had robbed him of any inner strength he may have had. His tone of voice suggested that whoever was upstairs was no danger to anyone. We mounted the stairs slowly; the door of the first bedroom on the landing was open. He was lying at the foot of the bed his head pointing towards the door. I will not go into detail, sufficient to say there was no need to take his pulse. He was, we discovered later, twenty-five years old. You will no doubt have witnessed the casual manner with which the TV detective drops to one knee and casually places his finger on the neck of the body, raises an eyebrow then returns to his feet shaking his head. They tried to teach me how to take a pulse like that in first aid, I am glad I never had to do it for real. I started forward into the room, Geoff placed a hand on my shoulder and I saw what he had already observed. The shotgun was propped against the wall several feet from the body.

'There's one thing for sure, Sarge', he said, 'he didn't put it there.' There was, as Eric Morecambe used to say, 'no answer to that'. We retraced our steps back down the stairs. I picked up a chair from the table and put it in front of the old man and sat down.

'Have you,' I asked gently, 'been upstairs?' We waited for the reply, this was not a time for haste.

'Aye, after the shot.' He paused and we waited.

'He was lying on the floor and the gun was across his legs.' He paused again. I waited, any pressure I reasoned could stop the flow altogether.

'I picked it up and broke it open.' My own thoughts took over for a second, that was what a farmer would do, make sure the gun was safe, an automatic reaction. I was aware he still talking.

'There was only the one shell in it. I took it out.'

'What did you do with it?' He nodded towards the fire.

'I threw it in the fire.' Geoff reached for the fire tidy and took up the poker and shovel; he raked about in the embers and out came what remained of the shotgun cartridge. I spoke again.

'Was there anyone else in the house?' He leaned back in the chair slightly as if to relieve an aching back.

'Just Mother, she ran straight out.' A suddenly anxious Geoff spoke up.

'Where has she gone?' The old man was obviously not as concerned as Geoff.

'She'll have gone to the daughter's, it's just down the road.' Geoff looked at me and raised an eyebrow and said,

'Mother?' He was several years younger than me with much less service and was obviously not familiar with the term. I had heard older married men in the colliery villages use the term when referring to their wives. I was never sure whether it was a term of endearment or recognition of her status in the home. I never heard wives referring to their husband as 'Father'. There was a telephone on the sideboard, a grudging acknowledgement of the modern world. I picked it up and spoke to Eric. Geoff took my place on the chair and began, very gently, to probe.

'Has he been upset about anything?' The old man answered another question as people in these circumstances often do.

'He's always been a quiet lad even as a young 'un, never bothered other bairns, never went out anywhere much, he's been worse as he grew up, he has never been off the place for a few weeks hardly out of the house. He came in today and went straight upstairs then the gun went off.' He lapsed into silence and closed his eyes it was as if he suddenly felt terribly tired.

Eric, always at his best on such occasions, soon had everything under control. Police Doctor who confirmed what we already knew, Scientific Aids took photographs, carefully removed the shotgun, DI and Superintendent asked questions and having satisfied themselves that everything that had to be done had been done, departed with a 'Well done.' Anne, policewoman, arrived having collected mother and daughter. The daughter collapsed in tears, 'Mother' sat down in the chair vacated by Geoff and gently took hold of her husband's hand. Neither spoke. Their grief, I thought, was not something that they would want to share with others. The undertaker came and went, taking their boy with him. We lingered a little longer feeling quite useless, we finally left with the usual offers of help should any be required. They said we had been very good but were obviously wanting us to go. I went on leave the following week.

When I returned I decided to go and see them; I asked Geoff if he would like to go with me. He said he had already been and saw no point in going back, which surprised me. They said it was kind of me to call and Mother made tea, but it was obvious that I was intruding. I knew now why Geoff did not want to go back. I left as soon as I politely could. If I was a psychologist I would be able to explain it better but to put it in modern idiom it was as if from the moment that shot went off they had gone on to auto-pilot. When, or indeed if ever, they resumed full control once more I cannot say, I never saw them again.

CHAPTER 17

Mrs McGarry's Boys

Eleven p.m. and I was working double with Ted at the bottom end of the town; much of it had been condemned and was awaiting the bulldozer. We were approaching Alexander Street, a row of dilapidated Victorian terrace houses, with a narrow back street and small back yards, with six-foot high brick walls, which you kept away from in case a brick fell on your head. An elderly man came hurrying around the corner and on seeing us, a smile of relief (always a sign of trouble in store) flitted across his face. The McGarry boys, he informed us, were at it again and this time they looked like killing each other.

The McGarry boys – Leo and Dennis – were both in their early forties and lived with their mother, who could have been anywhere between sixty and a hundred years old. Both had the same short, stocky build and vile temper. No one could remember a Mr McGarry – it was thought he had long since given up what he clearly believed to be an unequal struggle between himself, his wife and her lovely boys and departed for parts unknown. The boys made a precarious living harvesting sea coal. Most of their spare time seemed to be spent consuming unbelievable amounts of the local nectar (which was brewed just along the road) and fighting each other.

We headed, reluctantly, for Alexander Street, pausing at the police box on the corner to let the office know where we were going, a well-advised precaution when dealing with the McGarrys. The McGarry house was near the bottom end of the terrace and as we made our way down the street, we could see one of the boys (it turned out to be Dennis) rolling on the ground, while Leo was doing his best to use him as a football. Fortunately, he was wearing his welly boots (standard sea-coaling issue). Dennis was grasping a flat iron with which he was endeavouring to break Leo's legs as they came towards him. The movements would have turned a ballet choreographer green with envy.

Mrs McGarry, unlaced shoes over unstockinged feet, her skinny frame wrapped in an overall whose colours had long ago merged into a greasy blackish grey, seeing our somewhat tardy approach, exhorted us to hasten to quell the strife (or words to that effect). She had a masterly command of abusive language but it is inappropriate to repeat it here. As we got close to the battle, Leo gave Dennis a last kick and ran for the house. I went to get Dennis back on his feet, praying that he would not need hospital attention (the most experienced of nursing staff blanched at the thought of disrobing a McGarry). Ted, who was always inclined to dash in where angels fear to tread, started to follow Leo into the house – the smell would have put most people off.

As Ted neared the door, Leo reappeared, grasping a large earthenware teapot without which, in those days, no home was complete. Any illusions Ted may have harboured about being offered a conciliatory cup of tea were swiftly shattered as Leo threw the teapot at him. The pot hit Ted on the side of the head and he staggered backwards into my arms. Leo disappeared into the house, reappearing seconds later, waving a poker – not the sort we see

gracing the side of your coal-effect gas fire. This was the type made
by the lads on night-shift at the steel works for 'two bob' (two
shillings). About two feet long and half-an-inch around, it was a
fearsome weapon. I was wondering what I should do with Ted – it
was no use appealing to Leo's sense of fair play – he had none. I need
not have worried – the sight of that poker did wonders for Ted's
powers of recuperation.

We started to back-pedal rapidly, at the same time pulling out
those pitiful pieces of wood dignified with the title of 'truncheon'.
Seeing this sign of naked aggression gave Leo pause for thought.
Thankfully, he could not see my knees trembling beneath my
greatcoat and he decided to make a tactical withdrawal into the
house. We followed carefully, even though we did not think the
McGarrys could run to two teapots. This time I went first – it seemed
the decent thing to do. Leo went straight through the house and out
the back door. Ted ran out and around the back. I took a minute to
lock the back door and also point out to Dennis that we would not
be best pleased if he let Leo back in. Blood, where the McGarrys
were concerned, was definitely thicker than water. I galloped off after
Ted and found him skipping about the back street, dodging the
pieces of old bike frame that Leo was throwing over the yard wall –
sea-coaling was hard on bikes.

We decided that enough was enough – one way or another, Leo
was going to get his come-uppance. We would kick the yard door
open and hopefully, grab Leo before he realised what was happening.
Now usually kicking doors open is strictly for the 'telly' where the
doors are made of plywood and half-sawn through. However, this was
a very ancient and weary door that had seen a good deal of hard
knocks over far too many years. Leo appeared to be out of
ammunition and was busy hurling abuse over the wall. We stepped
forward and simultaneously kicked at the door. The door did not
move but the door frame did. It collapsed inward, taking the whole of
the door and a considerable amount of wall with it. Fortunately, some
of it fell on Leo (no lasting damage) – we charged through the dust and
debris, dragged Leo out and had the handcuffs on him in a trice (fear
lends wings). We dragged him, fighting, around into the front street.

The cavalry, in the shape of the Divisional car (despatched by a
kindly and thoughtful Sergeant) driven by Allen, whose fourteen

stone of bone and muscle were ever a welcome sight in times of trouble, was on its way down the street.

Mrs McGarry was exhorting the neighbours, who had gathered in friendly manner to watch the show (not many people had television then), to witness the way in which a heartless constabulary were treating her boy (or words to that effect!) Dennis (blood and water again) was rapidly working himself up to being a one-man rescue party. We threw Leo into the car and departed. We knew from experience that the Sergeant would not be looking forward to seeing Leo – taking Dennis as well would not have made him a happy man and we had to live with him. Ted was despatched to outpatients for a couple of stitches and given the rest of the week on light duties (office runabout).

The Sergeant gave me a quarter of an hour for a cup of tea and a smoke (as I have already said, a kindly and thoughtful man). This was, of course, in the days before stress had been invented.

CHAPTER 18

The Shooting

I WAS TAKING ADVANTAGE OF A pleasant summer afternoon to do a bit of gardening. The office window opened and Margaret handed the telephone out.

'It's Albert' (Town Office).

'Hello, Albert.'

'We've had a three-nine call, Ray, from Mr H at Railway Cottages. He says his neighbour has been shooting at him. His neighbour Albert is well into his seventies and spends his days propped up in bed with an oxygen mask strapped to his face. I'll have a look down.'

Railway Cottages were on the outskirts of the village – a bit isolated. Mr H was thin, weasel-faced and had never been known to work. His wife always looked miserable. No-one liked him and everyone pitied her. Their neighbours were an elderly couple who kept themselves to themselves. They both had a gentle, courteous manner and despite being reserved, were well-liked.

I arrived to find an indignant Mr H displaying two small bruises on his upper right arm, inflicted, he said, by his neighbour shooting at him whilst he was in the garden. He had no idea why he should do such a thing. I went to the adjoining cottage. The door was opened by Mrs B, the marks of tears still on her face. We neither of us spoke as she led me into the front room. Mr B was in his usual position on the single bed next to the window, which looked out onto the garden and was always slightly open.

'Can you tell me about it?' He nodded. I gently removed the oxygen mask.

'He has been nasty to her while I was in hospital, shouting about the garden fence and the weeds growing into his garden. I heard him again today and I thought I would give him a fright, so I shot at him through the window. I did not mean to hurt him.' He started to fight for breath, so I replaced the mask.

'Where's the gun?' She pointed to a cupboard at the other end of the room.

'I put it back in there where it belongs.'

'How did he get it?'

'God knows. I heard the bang and found him lying on top of the bed, with the gun beside him, trying to get his mask back on.' It was a small-bore single-barrelled shotgun – so rust-covered it was a wonder it had not blown up in his face; on an adjoining shelf a dust-covered tin, with two more cartridges. I picked them up, told them not to worry (as if that would help) and left. I had a brief word with Mr H, pointing out to him the desirability of keeping away from his neighbours and how annoyed I would be if he didn't. I called at the doctor's on the way home. He heard my story and shook his head in disbelief.

'The effort should have killed him.'

'Will he ever be fit enough to go to court, doctor?'

'I expect him going before the judge any time, Ray, but not the one you are thinking about. Call at the surgery in the morning; I'll have a letter for you.'

I walked into the office just in time to answer the phone. It was Albert.

'It's the DI, Ray, he wants to know what's going on.'

'Tell him it's all right, Albert – he did shoot at him but I have sorted it. I'll have a report in the morning.' Five minutes later, the phone rang again – this time it was the DI. Had I, he enquired gently, never heard of attempted murder or such minor offences as discharging a firearm with intent to injure and the desirability of submitting crime reports immediately in such matters? I told him my story; there was a brief pause.

'All right, Ray, but first thing in the morning.' I appeared in his office at 10 a.m., my report in a nice new brown folder.

'Sit down.' I sat down while he read through the report and the doctor's letter. He finished it and placed it back in the folder.

'What about this neighbour?' I told him my opinion of Mr H.

'Where's the gun and cartridges?'

'In the property cupboard.' He fingered the report.

'Leave it with me.' I stood up to go; he stopped me.

'You'll have had a word with that neighbour.'

'Yes, sir.' He nodded and I left.

Mr B went before his Judge a fortnight later. I put in an oral plea for leniency; I'm sure it was heard.

CHAPTER 19

The Flying Truncheon

WE WERE ON NIGHT-SHIFT, Tom and I. The half night-shift were home and tucked up in bed. So, we had the town to ourselves. We were short-handed in those days as well. We were on adjoining beats, sharing the same pillar at which to make our points. Tom was on the odd hour, I was on the even. Those pillars were at the sharp end of technology: about four-foot high, with a square box on top. At one side of the box was a door that members of the public could pull open. The switch-board operator was alerted by a bell; he would then converse with the supplicant as it were; on the other side was a door that could only be opened with a key and we all had one. This revealed a telephone with which we could converse with the switchboard operator without the rest of the town knowing what we were talking about. That switchboard was an awesome piece of equipment – about three-foot square, placed vertically against the wall, in front a sort of shelf from which protruded plugs that were attached to cables. You pushed one plug into the caller and the other into whoever they wished to talk to. In busy periods it looked like a spider's web – it was quite easy for the inexperienced to pull out or insert the wrong plug. On those occasions the amount of grief you got depended entirely on the rank of person you had disconnected.

I had just made my four o'clock point, where I had been visited by the Inspector and Sergeant. They had departed for the office and a cup of tea; I had tucked myself into a shop doorway in a side street, for a smoke. The sound of breaking glass came from the main street. It is always difficult to locate the origin of sound in the quiet of the night. I hurried to the end of the side street and peered round the corner. About twenty yards up the street I saw a shadowy figure in a shop doorway. No wireless in those days to call for assistance – you were on your own. I made my way towards the shop, trying to keep in what shadow I could find. The figure moved and I realised it was Tom. I hurried up to him; he was bent slightly forward, absolutely motionless, staring at the door as if in a hypnotic trance.

'What's happened?' He seemed to have lost the power of speech. His right hand came up and pointed at the door. I moved closer and saw that one of the glass panes in the door was broken.

'What's happened?' Tom's finger stabbed again at the door and I took a closer look. There on the floor, just inside the door, was a police truncheon. I presumed it was Tom's – I was right.

'How did that happen?' I realised that I was beginning to sound like an illiterate parrot.

'I was spinning it on my finger and it just flew off.'

There was a rising note of panic in Tom's voice. I knew what he meant – we had all done it. Sometimes we would have a competition to see who could spin it the fastest. You put your index finger through the truncheon strap and began slowly to revolve it around your finger, gradually building up speed. It had been known to cause burn marks on the finger. I remembered reading that the weight of a missile was increased by its velocity or something like that. That poor little pane of glass must have thought it had been hit by a bus – not a lot of double-glazing or armoured glass about in those days.

Tom came alive.

'How am I going to get it out?' There was no doubt about the panic in his voice this time. I had a sudden flash of genius (I did not get many – still don't). They were carrying out slum clearance in the next street and there were all sorts of bits of wire and wood. I departed at what could only be described as a brisk pace. I returned a few minutes later, breathless but triumphant, with a length of wire. The end was swiftly turned into a hook; Tom inserted it into the window, hooked it into the truncheon strap and drew it towards the hole. It was then that we realised that the truncheon had gone through the window vertically and would only return the same way. I took out my truncheon and gently tapped the piece of glass between two cracks that radiated from the hole. The piece dropped out beautifully, enough to allow finger and thumb to be inserted and the truncheon lifted off the wire and through the hole.

It was only then that we realised we were going blue through not breathing. We started up again. Our relief was short-lived when we realised that we now had to find an explanation for that hole. They say God is good to fools and lovers. We were both married, so were a bit of each. There in the gutter lay a piece of stone that could have been made to measure. It was carefully dropped through the hole. I went off to return the piece of wire and Tom to the pillar to report the damage. The key-holder duly attended. Tom expressed the opinion that the stone could have been thrown up by the tyre of a passing motor vehicle (it was not original and had been used before).

Well, it was better than criminal damage and it kept the crime figures down, which pleased everyone, from the Detective Inspector through to the Home Secretary. The Sergeant agreed with Tom's opinion – well, by this time it was 5 a.m. and he was thinking of his bed.

I do hope this little story will discourage our young policemen from trying a 'John Wayne' spin with their machine pistols – one dreads to think of the damage they could cause.

CHAPTER 20

George

He was in his late sixties when I knew him. Six-foot tall, usually clad (you could never say dressed) in an ex-army greatcoat, worn belted in winter and as a sort of flowing cloak in summer. A pair of ex-army boots on his feet in winter, shoes in summer and a trilby hat of indeterminate age and colour on his head. What he had been in his younger days, I never knew but then he was a tramp. Tramps were still a fairly common sight in those days, walking their chosen route. They did not, as popular myth would have it, wander all over the countryside 'willy nilly' but stuck to certain well-defined routes between their chosen towns or cities. The same hostels were visited on a regular basis and in between, there were houses where tea-cans were willingly filled and very often a sandwich or 'bit of dinner' provided. In summer there were certain barns and out-houses and in winter a warm corner could be found at the brick ovens, steelworks or colliery yard, where a kindly night-shift would turn a blind eye and often provide a sandwich and bedtime fag.

It was the weekend before Christmas and Bill was on the bottom beat, which took in one of the main shopping streets. He was not long out of training school and it was his first night-shift on his own. An ice-laden wind was blowing up the street straight off the North Sea. His head shrunk down into his shoulders, buried as far as possible into his greatcoat collar, left hand clutching a torch buried deep inside his coat pocket, whilst his right hand darted out at regular intervals checking the shop doors. You checked your fronts first and then the backs. In those days we thought Pandas were furry little black and white bears that lived in China.

Bill came to a door that was set back in a deep porch way. He stepped inside to check the door and recoiled as a dark shadow moved. He need not have worried – it was only George. He had had a drink and was no doubt now contemplating the two-mile walk to the steelworks and the hole in the perimeter fence. Loitering in shop doorways at night was not allowed. Bill, who had never met George before, pointed this out to him but then moved on without any attempt to enforce the rule. As he said later, he would not have turned a dog out on such a bitter night, although the Sergeant did not seem to be at all troubled when he turned him out.

'Lock us up drunk, son,' said George. Bill ignored him and carried on. He had only gone a few yards when there came the unmistakeable sound of breaking glass. He hurried back to find George gazing ruefully down at a large hole in the bottom glass panel of the shop door. George was 'locked up drunk' and spent the weekend in the luxury of the cells.

On the Monday morning, I was on 9 a.m. to 5 p.m. court duty, a 'cushy number'. I collected George from the cells and took him up the stairs to court. The court consisted of three magistrates, the chairman – a prominent local businessman; the magistrates clerk, a tubby, bad-tempered, ill-mannered man who no-one liked (although we did wonder about his mother) – his false teeth rattled alarmingly when he was agitated and had to be sucked back into place. The Chief Inspector was in charge of prosecutions (we rarely employed a solicitor in those days). I brought George before the Bench. The clerk asked him for his name, which George willingly supplied. He then read out the charge and asked George if he pleaded guilty or not guilty. George, to no-one's surprise, said he was guilty. The Chief Inspector read out the evidence. At the conclusion, the clerk asked George if he had anything to say before the Magistrate pronounced sentence.

'Could you put us away over Christmas, sir?' said George. The Chief Inspector developed a nasty cough. The clerk's short fuse exploded:

'The Machistrates,' he barked through teeth tight-clenched to minimise the rattle, 'are not here to provide you with accommodashun over Christmas.' There followed a quick 'shuck' as the teeth were brought back under control. The two flanking magistrates appeared to have found something very interesting on their notepads. The chairman, being made of sterner stuff, gazed coldly down at George for a moment. He leaned forward and beckoned the Chief Inspector. He then leaned over the bench as close as he could get to the Chief Inspector – obviously what he was about to say was not meant for general consumption. I carefully moved a step nearer and put my ears on full alert.

'How much money has he?'

'Half-a-crown, sir.' The Chairman sat back in his chair and fixed George with a cold gaze.

'There can be no excuse for this sort of behaviour – there will be a fine of five pounds or two weeks imprisonment. There will be no time allowed for payment.'

George's lips began to move. Before he could speak, I had gripped him firmly by the elbow and walked him out of court. I was sure the Chairman would prefer to take his thanks as read. A few hours later, I collected George from the cells where he had feasted royally on sausage and mash provided by the caretaker's wife, who was paid the princely sum of half-a-crown for 'prisoners' dinners'. He was smoking a full-size cigarette – a rare luxury – and he had a further ten in his tin. We had had a whip-round – a fag a man. We strolled companionably out to the prison van. As I was closing the door, George put his hand on it.

'Thanks, son, Merry Christmas.'

'That's all right, George. Merry Christmas.'

CHAPTER 21

Chicken Run

I T WAS ONE OF THOSE DEEPLY silent winter nights when the cold was so intense it reached into your bones. Bob and Zelda (the dog) were doubled up with Jack, the local beat man on 'poultry watch'. In those somewhat far-off days, in the days around Christmas and New Year you were sent to stand at some god-forsaken crossroads in the middle of nowhere to stop and check vehicles for stolen poultry. It wasn't as if there were many vehicles about. You were lucky to see half a dozen in the two hours you were on (usually between 10 p.m. and 12 midnight) and they were usually locals well known to the local 'poliss' who invariably was one of the team. Many of them were local farmers on their way home from a quiet pint at the local pub. The cars did not so much stop as pause. The car window would be somewhat begrudgingly wound down a few inches and as you leaned forward you were met by a blast of beer laden breath tinged with stale tobacco.

'All reet lads? You're doing a grand job, gooneet.' The tail-lights disappeared into the distance. Occasionally we did stop a vehicle driven by some farmer or local butcher who was making a late delivery of oven-ready poultry. The occupant would ask us, with tears in his eyes, not to tell his wife that that we had caught him with a naked 'bird' in his car then drive on convulsed with laughter. I never heard of anyone being caught. However we were told it was a deterrent and we were big on deterrents in those days. Well, it made life so much easier, deterring was always easier than detecting. So you stood there freezing, fighting off the cold by drinking from your flask of hot tea (to which a loving wife had added a 'drop of something extra') whilst hopefully deterring.

Their shift being over, Bob dropped a grateful Jack back home and continued on 'mobile patrol'.

'You lads,' said the Chief Inspector, I/C Dog Section, 'should not be smoking or using your heater in your vans, it effects the nose of your dog and reduces its effectiveness in detecting scent.' Bob reflected on the fact that the Chief Inspector would by now be tucked up in bed and the chances of Zelda having to use her nose that night were not very great so he leaned forward and switched on the heater.

It was about 1 p.m. when the call came through. A farmer returning from one of the many 'balls' held at this time of the year (farmers, grocers, police, butchers etc. they were always 'balls', never dances, gentlemen in evening dress, who never smoked until after the loyal toast, and ladies in their 'gowns') had disturbed someone in his chicken pen. Bob, fortunately not too far away, was quickly on the scene. He found the farmer hopping from foot to foot and cursing. Bob did not know whether this was because he had had his chicken pen raided or the fact that he had broken through the ice on a very obnoxious puddle with his brightly polished evening shoes.

Zelda, who had a great reputation for her nose, thankfully unaffected by the heater and eager to use it was released from the van. Bob, pausing only to put on his gloves and turn up his coat collar put on her tracking harness and away they went. The conditions were perfect, chummy's number nines had crushed the frost tipped grass perfectly. The track led across the fields to the old mineral line railway from thence to the back street of the nearby village. Halfway up the back street Zelda paused then turned into a back yard. The back kitchen light was on. Fortunately the curtains had not been fully drawn.

Bob tiptoed forward and applied his eye to the slight gap. Chummy was sitting with the now dead cock chicken on his knee and in the act of plucking it. What to do – banging on the door and shouting 'police' was not going to do any good, chummy would soon be up and gone. In those days we had not been issued with the battering rams they now use to break a door down and anyway it might wake up the bairns and disturb the neighbours. Bob tapped gently but persistently at the door. He was rewarded with, 'Wha's that?' Bob replied in a husky whisper with the immortal words,

'It's me, man, open the door, hurry up.' The door was duly opened the rest as they say is history. My father often said that low cunning always beat brute force on this occasion at least he was right.

CHAPTER 22

Working Mates

WE WERE ON NIGHT-SHIFT, the city had quietened down so we had moved out into the outlying villages to check 'vulnerable property', all those Co-op Stores and Working Men's Clubs. Rebel (the dog) had jumped in the front of the van with me so he could be out quickly if required instead of having to wait for me coming around to open the back door. On those occasions when we met one of our 'detached beat' colleagues doing their late rounds they would open the door and ask,

'All right, Rebel?' He would reply by shoving a wet nose into their outstretched hand. Sometimes they would ask him if he would mind hopping in the back so we could give them a ride around their patch before dropping them off at home, sometimes we would be asked to keep an eye on certain property, or look out for a certain vehicle or person. We always obliged. Bait time found us in the Sub-Divisional office. Rebel was always welcome, he was considered a part of the shift. He was also a useful depository for rejected sandwiches. Rebel did not reject anything. He was often asked for his opinion if the bait-time debate got a little heated. One of the protagonists would ask,

'What do you think of that, Rebel?' He would rouse himself from the comatose position he adopted at bait-time, gaze around at the assembled company then flop back down again. There would be a shout of,

'There you are, Rebel thinks its rubbish.'

It was 3 a.m. when the radio crackled into life. A 999 call, a wagon seen being driven out of a local builders' yard. We were only about a mile away so were quickly on the scene. As we drove into the back street where the yard was situated we saw the wagon halfway out of the yard blocking the street. We jumped out of the van, I checked the cab whilst Rebel made a quick circuit of the wagon which was full of scrap copper, obviously someone was after making a quick bob. There was never a need for words on these occasions, he seemed to know better than me what was required. I am told that the

American Space Agency have been experimenting with telepathy as a means of communicating in space. Rebel and I had it off to a fine art all those years ago. There was no one in sight. Rebel disappeared into the yard. I started to follow when there was a sudden shout followed by the sound of Rebel interrogating a suspect. I ran into the yard, there was no sign of anyone. Then I realised that the noise was coming from the bottom of a flight of steps leading to a lower level of the yard. Chummy was half lying half kneeling at the bottom of the steps with Rebel standing over him carrying out his interrogation. I told him to desist. Ever obedient he backed off at least six inches and reduced his voice to a deep growl. I bent over chummy.

'What happened?'

'That b★★★★y dog knocked me down the steps.' The growl deepened. Rebel objected to being referred to as 'that dog' let alone 'that b★★★★y dog'.

'You should have stood still.'

'Ah didn't get the b★★★★y chance did I.' I was helping him to his feet when I heard the sound of running feet. The cavalry in the shape of traffic patrol had arrived. I shouted a warning:

'Stand still, the dog's working.' The footsteps came to an abrupt stop. Everyone knew how upset Rebel could get if anyone interrupted him when making an arrest. Rebel trotted up to the top of the steps and gazed down the yard. The traffic lads were quick to reassure him.

'It's us, Rebel.' He nodded them through. They were careful to keep out of the way as he escorted his prisoner to the van. They offered to wait for the owner of the yard and sort the wagon out. It transpired that chummy worked at the yard as wagon driver and was putting in a bit of unofficial overtime to enhance his wages. We returned to the Sub-Div. Office where Rebel presented his prisoner to the Sergeant.

'What have you got here, Rebel?' Rebel, never one for explanations, let me do the talking. He was just as happy to let me do the paper work. Once that was completed we set off for the Div. Office and the cells. The Inspector greeted us.

'He's walking funny,' nodding at chummy.

'Ah hurt me knees.' He lifted up both trouser legs showing two skinned knees.

'He must have done it when they fell down the steps.' The Inspector looked at me with consternation.

'Is Rebel all right?'

'He's fine. What about him?'

'You can get the doctor to him when he is in the cells, come on, Rebel.' Rebel followed him happily out to the front office and the biscuit tin. The office man having been asked to summon the doctor we left for home. We stopped for a walk in a field and made ourselves comfortable before going to bed. Rebel stopped, as he always did, to give me a quick nuzzle before jumping into his kennel.

The next day I had a phone call from a delighted CID. They had paid a visit to chummy's allotment shed and found a treasure-trove of building materials. Obviously this was not his first nocturnal expedition. The DI was very pleased, the contents of that shed did wonders for his detected figures.

The other day I had a talk with our local policeman. He tried to explain to me such things as pre-active policing and pro-active policing, community policing and core policing, crime management and so on. I am sure it is all very necessary but in those far-off days we just policed together, including Rebel, it seemed to work very well. I hope you will not think me over-sentimental but I often think of Rebel and wish he were back. He was one of the best mates I have had.

CHAPTER 23

The Gunman

WE DID NOT HAVE ARMED PROTECTION units or rapid response vehicles. We did have a Humber Hawk saloon, side valve, and an Austin van but neither could be described as 'rapid'. To be fair there was no great call for guns and just as well. We did have a truncheon and handcuffs but both were concealed in special pockets, it would not do to flaunt them in public. I was once reprimanded by the Inspector for letting my truncheon strap appear out of my pocket. Did I, he asked, want to panic the public by letting them see this sign of aggression? It does not seem to bother the public these days as our young policemen stroll around with their revolvers and machine pistols. Our training sergeant told us that truncheons were only to be drawn *in extremis*. One of the main reasons, he said, was that someone

75

might take it off you and wallop you with it. The other was that if you did draw your truncheon you would have to submit a report justifying your action. We did of course have weapons, usually ex-army revolvers. They were kept in a locked cupboard in the Superintendent's office only to be issued by the Superintendent after he had obtained the Chief Constable's permission. The recipient, who had to sign for the gun and ammunition, had to account for any ammunition used, which I imagine could prove a little embarrassing. 'It's in the body sir,' was usually the response an officer who had had experience of such things in the armed forces. We were told that if we were faced with an armed man (we never envisaged an armed woman) we were to keep cool and use our initiative. When I encountered an armed man that is just what I did. Unfortunately despite my singular act of courage no one thought to award me a medal.

I was on early days; it was a lovely summer morning. I strolled out of the police station feeling at peace with the world. The only other occupant of the street was a short, stocky man with, despite the warmth of the morning, an anorak zipped up to his chin and a woolly hat pulled down to his eyebrows. Just a workman on his way to work. I turned and walked down the street. I heard a shout.

'Hey, Poliss, just a minute I want a word.' As I was the only 'poliss' on the street I decided the words were meant for me. I turned around and my blood, as they say, turned to ice. Woolly hat was walking towards me with a gun in his right hand, which was pointing at me. I searched frantically for my initiative without any success. I then heard a squeaky voice, which I later realised was mine, say,

'Yes lad what can I do for you?'

'I've found this,' said woolly hat, waggling the gun at me. I spoke with a sense of relief.

'Well don't point it at me.' He looked at it for a moment then promptly pointed it at his foot. I walked slowly forward and took the gun from him holding it by the butt and avoiding the trigger. I walked back to the office followed by woolly hat. I knew nothing about guns but had no worries on that score; the Sergeant and Geoff (town office) had both been in the war and no doubt had a working knowledge of firearms. When I laid the gun on the office counter the Sergeant gazed at it for a moment and said,

'Where did you get it?' I nodded at woolly hat.

'He found it.' The Sergeant looked at it a little longer and then said,

'Is it loaded?' I looked at him in amazement.

'I don't know, I thought you would with being in the war.'

'I was flight engineer on a Wellington bomber,' said the Sergeant with some indignation. 'I didn't go around shooting folk.' His tone of voice suggested that dropping bombs on people was not like shooting them. (A bit like the man who fires the cruise missile somewhat remote from the result of his action.) 'Geoff should know, he was in the Coldstream Guards.' Geoff inspected the gun, he gazed at it for a moment and said,

'Is it loaded?' It was the Sergeant's turn to be amazed.

'You should know,' he said to Geoff, 'you were in the Guards!'

'I was a tank driver,' Geoff replied, 'another fella fired the gun and it was a lot bigger one than this.' I turned towards the Inspector's office.

'I wouldn't ask him, he spent the war in the Intelligence Corps evaluating information other people got; come to think of it he is still doing it.' This from the Sergeant, he and the Inspector were not on the best of terms.

At this point woolly hat spoke up like a man who was fast running out of patience.

'Can I go, I'm late for work.' Geoff retrieved the found property book from under the counter.

'You'll have to wait till I fill this in.'

It was then that the Inspector appeared, no doubt to find out what all the noise was about. He saw the revolver, gazed at it thoughtfully then looked over Geoff's shoulder at the form he was filling in. Seemingly satisfied he picked up the revolver strolled across to the office safe and popped it in before locking the door and dropping the keys in front of the Sergeant.

'Give headquarters a ring for the firearms expert', he said, before returning to his office.

'I suppose,' said Geoff to know one in particular, 'that's why he was in the Intelligence Corps.'

CHAPTER 24

The Grahams

I T WAS ABOUT 2.30 P.M. Ian was wandering along one of the terrace streets that made up two-beat defending the Queen's Peace. Not that there was a great deal to defend, although I remembered an old and experienced Sergeant in my probationer days telling me on a particular cold and rainy morning that there was no telling what 'they' might be getting up too if I was not out and about. Two-beat was a quiet area consisting of terrace housing, a builder's yard, the local allotments and a corner shop. The corner shop was owned and run by Ali. I never knew, to my shame, if that was his proper name. He was of Asian origin, a quiet courteous man, his wife a gentle lady and their children the best mannered in the area. On the odd occasions when I called in his shop for an ounce of tobacco he would tell me that,

'I only charge you wholesale price Sergeant.' Which meant I got my tobacco a few pence cheaper. He never asked and I am sure he never expected any favours and I never felt in any way corrupted, it was just something which he wished to do and it would I felt be ungracious to refuse.

It was the man from 'the Pru' who approached Ian. There was, he said, something funny going on at number five, number five being the home of the Graham family, two brothers and a sister, all of whom, through some quirk of nature were of low intelligence. According to the neighbours they were 'well short of a full shilling'. In these days this would not be deemed to be politically correct but nevertheless summed up the Grahams perfectly. Nevertheless they kept themselves reasonably clean and tidy and did the same for their home. They also had one of the best gardens in the allotments. George and Harry were both in their fifties (they were never in real employment but got the odd labouring job) whilst Sara, with her sparse hair, skinny frame and lined face could have been anything from fifty upwards. The neighbours liked them, the lads were always willing to help out with odd jobs that needed doing and were generous with their ample garden produce. Sara helped out with cleaning jobs.

The man from the Pru said there was no sign of George and when he had enquired about him Harry had simply said that George had stopped in bed. Ian promised to call in, which he did. Harry was sat in front of the fire whilst Sara was cleaning up. He asked about George. Harry said that he was still in bed.

'Our Sara has taken him some dinner in but he never spoke to her.' Ian wandered into the front room which served as a third bedroom. There were two trays of food on the dressing table, breakfast and dinner, Ian presumed. George was sat up reclining on his pillows. He looked, said Ian, very comfortable; unfortunately he was also very dead. Which, said Ian, who never lost his wonderful sense of humour no matter the situation, would account for his loss of appetite. Ian alerted Eric and the machine went smoothly into gear. I joined Ian. The doctor attended to tell us what we already knew: George, he thought had left us sometime during the night. The Co-op undertaker came and went, taking George with him. The neighbours, kindly folk, rallied round. I talked to Sara and Harry to try and explain, gently, what was going on. They were more bemused than bereaved. Sara said 'he had niver been poorly,' as if a reasonable period of illness was a prerequisite to dying. Harry shook his head and said 'he had niver said owt.' As if he thought that George really should have made them aware of his intention to shuffle off this mortal coil. Social Services were sent for and came. As an extra precaution I instructed Ian to watch over them until inquest and burial were over, he did not really need telling.

The funeral was the following week, it was on the morning and we were 'early days' so Ian and I slipped into the back of the church. The Grahams were accompanied by a caring woman from Social Services and those kindly neighbours had turned out. The vicar coped with what must have been a difficult task very gently. The Grahams just looked rather puzzled by it all. I popped into see them from time to time. Their life went on in the same way. They never mentioned George in the way that people usually speak of family who have died. It was if they did not believe he had really left them. I liked to think that they were right.

CHAPTER 25

The Poachers

SUNDAY AFTERNOON, WE HAD FRIENDS for tea and were about to sit down when the phone rang. It was one of my farmers. I did not like the man. I know all farmers had a reputation for being careful, something to do with their somewhat precarious profession so dependent on circumstances they could not control. This one was just plain greedy and of a miserable nature. He had, he said, just seen two men going across the Top Field obviously poaching and he wanted them reporting. I thought he should be grateful to get rid of some of the rabbits that infested his Top Field. I replaced the phone, apologised to the guests, wheeled out the motorbike and headed for open country. It was a pleasant summer's day, ideal for a walk in the fields and at any other time I would have enjoyed it. I parked the bike in a side lane, hopped over the hedge and walked along the hedge back. I was about fifty yards away when the Jack Russell alerted them. They did not bother to run, there was no point, and I knew them. They were decent lads in their late teens both working at the local colliery, out for a 'bit of sport'. I closed the gap.

'All right lads?'

'Yes, Mr Gibbon.' I looked at the two brand new nets stretched over the entrance to the rabbit burrow. 'The ferret still running?'

'Aye.'

'You had better take them nets up, can't have you catching Mr . . .'s rabbits. I wanted to add 'the miserable b★★★★r', but thought better not. Conversation temporarily exhausted, I lit my pipe and joined them in their vigil. My memory was jogged and I remembered when I was a lad my friends and I would go out rabbiting, not always on land where we had permission, to supplement the pocket money our mothers gave us out of our wages. In the daytime we would use the ferret, at night we would use the long net and dead dog. The catch was sold to the local butcher for 1s. (one shilling) each. That got you a night out. Nine pence for a seat in the pictures and two and a half pence for a packet of five Woodbines. A rabbit bolting out of the burrow like an express train interrupted my reverie, the Jack Russell registered a near miss, and the ferret appeared shortly after and was quickly popped into his bag. I remembered, gratefully, that when arresting poachers you could seize any equipment that did not bite. I wondered what sort of a fool would grab a blood-loving ferret and a feisty Jack Russell.

'I will need to take them nets but I've got the bike, so you will just have to drop me them some time.' I emphasised the 'some'. A few days later I returned home late in the evening to be told by Margaret that two lads had left two carrier bags, one containing two rather dilapidated nets, the other a rabbit prepared ready for the oven. I had no doubt they had acquired it quite lawfully, they did have permission to go on some farmers' land, and it would have been most ungracious to refuse it. I met one of their fathers later and he told me how annoyed he was at 'them letting the farmer see them and causing you so much trouble.' I agreed it was careless.

They appeared at the local magistrates court some three weeks later. Again it was a lovely sunny day. The prosecuting solicitor, a young man not long out of college, in later years held in great affection, noted for his sense of humour and absolute integrity, approached me with a worried look.

'The farmer is not here PC Gibbon.'

'He won't be, Mr . . ., he is busy with the harvest.'

'What happens if they are represented and find a reason to plead not guilty?' I gazed at him wondering how best I could explain these matters to this young man.

'These are local lads,' I said, 'properly brought up. They will not be represented and will be pleading guilty'. He returned to the solicitor's bench looking decidedly nervous. When brought before the court they pleaded guilty. The magistrates, two local miners and one local business man, were totally sympathetic and utterly biased (nobody liked that farmer). The chairman (one of the miners) pointed out to them the error of their ways, the fact that they were poaching on a Sunday; the fact that he was a good Methodist was mentioned. He then went on to fine them £5 each and ordered the confiscation of their nets.

That young solicitor had a good memory. I was introduced to him at a social function some eighteen months later. He smiled broadly and said,

'I know Mr Gibbon, he looks after poachers.'

I do not suppose the young policemen of today do much in the way of poaching which is a great pity, it was a pleasant way of spending an afternoon, and, if done correctly did wonders for community relations.

APPENDIX

The Mayor's Bodyguard

The Mayor of Durham (whose full title is 'The Right Worshipful, The Mayor of Durham') has historically, the oldest Mayoral Body-guard outside the City of London, and is ranked equal fifth in precedence in the country behind York, Belfast, and Cardiff. Locally, the Mayor ranks after the Sovereign and his/her Lord Lieutenant for the County.

The full strength of the Bodyguard is fifteen. They pride themselves on having never failed to respond the Mayor's call to duty. The Bodyguard is one of the oldest institutions in the City of Durham, and dates back as far as the thirteenth century. In those days, they were called upon to protect the Warden of the City, who was appointed by the Trade Guilds, who governed, and carried out the work in the City. The Warden in his turn, appointed the Bodyguard, because there was no constabulary at that time. The wealthy Prince Bishops called upon the Warden and his Bodyguard to protect the City from marauders. The Wardens were also called upon to collect taxes, and the Bodyguard's duty was to protect the Warden from attack.

The first Mayor of Durham was appointed in 1602, and the real tradition of the Mayoral Bodyguard began at that time. The function of the Bodyguard in the seventeenth century was to collect taxes from the toll gates of the City. The proceeds went into civic coffers, but when the Mayor left office, so did this money. In Victorian times, the Bodyguard lost its 'tough' image, and took on a smart appearance: frock coats and top hats and carried long thin canes. The style of dress today consists of long black cloaks and Tudor style hats, each member of the Bodyguard carries a halbard (a long pole with a spike, combined with an axe head at its end). Some used today are original, dating back to the sixteenth century, and some are replicas. Originally, the halbards were used, together with the pikes, and held at an angle of 45 degrees, as a first line of defence in battle. Two of the Bodyguard carry staffs, which were the original implements used by the constables, appointed by the Wardens, in the days prior to the police force. The Captain of the Bodyguard carries a silver topped cane, with which he taps the timing of the march. The Bodyguard walk very slowly, taking very short paces, in time with the Captain. The Civic Sword and Mace are carried by special bearers, who do not belong to the Bodyguard. The Mace is always reversed in the presence of the Sovereign, because, as a symbol of the Mayor's authority, it becomes redundant in the presence of the Monarch. The Bodyguard hold an Annual Meeting on Mayor Making day (the day of the Annual meeting of the City Council) when the Captain is elected, and the Secretary to the Bodyguard deals with any vacancy, on which all members have a vote. New members of the Bodyguard are sworn in by the Mayor, in front of a meeting of the full Council of the City.

Each year, the Mayor chooses the colours of the rosettes, which are worn on the right side of the Bodyguard's headgear.

By kind permission of The City of Durham